THE ULTIMATE
ADVANTAGE

7 SIMPLE KEYS TO UNLEASH YOUR FULL POTENTIAL
AND LIVE AN EXTRAORDINARY LIFE

KOONAL JAIN

ISBN: 978-1-7352141-2-2

PERSONAL GROWTH / TRANSFORMATION

Editing by Ms. Shankhabela Mukherjee
Front Cover Design by Mrs. Shesha Poddar
Interior Art Work by M/s MediaZoma
Typeset by Mr. Indrajit Saha

First Edition printed in April, 2021

Published by:
Mind Spirit Works LLC
New Jersey, USA

Marketed by:
Book Corporation
R.N.Mukherjee Road
Kolkata, India

www.koonaljain.com

'SPECIAL BOOK BONUSES'

As a Thank-You for purchasing *The Ultimate Advantage*, Koonal Jain is offering "Free Book Bonuses".

If you're truly committed to 'Living The Extraordinary Life', be sure to visit www.theultimateadvantage.club and click on "Free Book Bonuses" to receive several valuable gifts that include :

1. A frame-worthy list of declarations that empowers you in cultivating a NO MATTER WHAT attitude.
2. A 'Holy-Grail' template to completely fall in love with your dreams and manifest them into reality.
3. 1-Page Daily Productivity Optimiser that helps you develop a laser-focus and get the most out of your day.
4. The 67-Day Habit Installation Challenge that gives you the authority to change any habit and make progress consistent and automatic.
5. The Ultimate Advantage 'Valuable Life Lessons'.

To the most important people in my life
My wife Neha and my daughter Amaira.

And to our parents
*Kiran and Sneh Prabha Jain, Raj and Suman,
Deepak and Manju, Raja and Ranu, Rakesh and Neelam*
for always believing in me inspite of my
imperfections and failures.

ACKNOWLEDGEMENT

Like everything else in life, any significant accomplishment requires the effort of many people, and this book is no different. As I sat down to think of the people I would like to thank and appreciate for their support in making this book possible, the list continued to grow.

First, I thank my wife, my family, and friends, whose patience and support was instrumental in helping me complete this book. They always received my ideas with an empathetic ear, which further encouraged me to keep on writing.

I can't thank my editor enough – Ms. Shankhabela Mukherjee, who hung in there with me in those final hours of last-minute changes.

Then, ofcourse, were the combined efforts of Ms. Aakanksha Surana and Mrs. Shesha Poddar (Cover Designer) and Ms. Kritika Jain and Mr. Anirudh Agarwal from Media Zoma (Graphic Designers) and Mr. Indrajit Saha (Type-setter) who gave the finishing touches to the book.

I am indebted to Ms. Sakshi Jain and Mr. Devesh Gourisaria for lending me their laptop to complete writing the book. (My computer crashed, and as I had no data back-up I had to rewrite the first 5 chapters all over again. Now I know the importance of a back up :))

Last but not least, I would also like to take the opportunity to thank various leaders and teachers whose character, persona, strategies and methods have inspired me. Every effort has been made to give credit where it is due for the examples, stories, content and anecdotes contained herein. If unintentionally I have omitted giving due credit, future editions will do so once they are brought to my notice.

FOREWORD

When Koonal Jain approached me to write the Foreword for The Ultimate Advantage, a book about 7 keys that claims to help transform people's lives, I was unsure what to expect. These days there are so many who write a book for the sake of writing it. But when I started going through the manuscript of Koonal's book, I was pleasantly surprised.

I found Koonal had a deep and profound understanding of human behaviour and the psychology of inspiration and achievement. He's a person who truly wants to help his fellow human beings learn how to use the power within them to create the life of their dreams that fulfils their aspirations.

Koonal is not talking about some mystical or other-worldly power, but about a practical set of strategies and tools that could enable human beings to tap into their potential. It could empower people to take effective action towards achieving their goals and aspirations, and most importantly, have a fulfilling life at the same time. I think this book can play a pivotal role in the field of human potential and achieving peak performance.

This book is cutting edge in its content and methodology. Koonal's perspective towards, among other things, potential, purpose and meaning of life, physical energy and persuasion are progressive and forward-looking. With these tools, one can feel confident to address various challenges in life. It is a must-read book for anyone who is dedicated to personal growth and excellence.

Reading this book would undoubtedly add to people's intellectual development insofar as personal growth and development are concerned. This book should help the readers implement the various tools and take their lives to a whole new and fulfilling level.

Narinder Kakar
'Professor Emeritus'
University for Peace and its,
Permanent Observer of the United Nations

CONTENTS

BEFORE YOU BEGIN

Dear Companion,

I congratulate you on your investment in this book and yourself. I sincerely respect and applaud you for taking a decision to raise your game and take your life to a whole new level.

You know what, even though I may have never met you, I believe I know who you are. You are someone who doesn't want to settle for anything less than what you deserve. And it is that very desire to excel that has made you curious to pick up this book.

What's more?

I know for a fact that no matter where you are in your life right now, you deserve much more given your potential.

And let me make a wild guess.

You already know it.

No matter how well you're already doing or how challenged your life may now be, deep down inside of you, lives a belief. A belief that you can do much more than what you are doing, and achieve significantly more than what you are achieving. You know that you can be outstanding and serve with excellence at whatever you do.

So, what's stopping you?

Change!

Fair enough, but you must have heard this a million times before.

It goes without saying that we're living in chaotic times where the world is experiencing lightning change. By the time you figure something out, something new crops up! Hence, it's become more important than ever to be ready to adapt, adopt and reorganise our way of living. It's required to not only keep pace with the change but also take advantage of the Tempo of Disruption that's become the 'new normal'.

It is my sheer privilege to provide the strategies, tools and insights that will help you tap into the unique gift that is already present within you. It will empower you to have access to the resources required to withstand the turbulent times ahead and fortify the mental and emotional bounce-back-ability necessary for the very foundation of a flourishing and fulfilling future.

This book is designed to awaken you by disrupting the way you perceive the world. It forces you to pause and think about key aspects of your life that may have been running on autopilot for years. But beware: Once you discover the patterns that this book brings to light, you cannot turn a blind eye to any of the happenings around you.

So, how does this book work?

Firstly, I would like to take the liberty to call this **NOT** a typical 'Self-Help book' but a comprehensive "**Training System**" put into a book. It helps you design a rewarding and fulfilling life by offering the tools and strategies you will need to unlock your full potential.

Also, this isn't just ONE book, but 7 "Training Systems" combined in one. I consider TIME (both yours and mine) a very precious resource. And I don't particularly appreciate reading self-help books that drag-out and use 60000 plus words to teach a relatively simple concept. I have no desire or intention to stretch out an idea to waste your time and belittle the trust you have bestowed upon me.

Hence, I've consciously attempted to provide enormous value in a detailed yet cohesive set of ideas packed with golden wisdom nuggets in a fun way (and most importantly) in minimal time.

A word of caution: The concepts presented in the book cannot be mastered by casual browsing or by cramming the whole book down in one reading. I would suggest you read it slowly and without distraction, one chapter at a time. And remember, repetition is the key to real learning. On that account, I wish this will be a book you'll read repeatedly and use it as a tool to activate yourself and discover the answers that already reside within you.

By all means, it's really up to you to decide how you want to go about this book. But, if you genuinely desire to extract the most and optimise your results, I recommend these strategies:

1. **Go all in:** When asked a question or to do an exercise, please take out the time to reflect/think and answer them. Please do take out time to explore choices, challenge your belief systems and prepare a blueprint for your life. Please do not ignore them, or else you may end up knowing things intellectually, but it may not result in any significant breakthroughs.

2. **Teach someone else:** According to research, you may retain approximately 90% of what you learn when you explain/teach the concept to someone else immediately. There's a good reason why. When you teach, it challenges and forces you to think, and it helps pinpoint the holes in your knowledge. So, if nothing else, teach or share with others for your own sake.

3. **Decide to Commit:** The ultimate aim of reading this book is to apply what you've learned when it matters the most. So, whenever you come across a concept that YOU think is valuable, highlight it and ask yourself **"How am I going to use it to improve the quality of my life?"** Make a note of the same (space provided at the end of the book – '*Key Takeaways*') and commit to taking immediate action. Remember, you will either use it or lose it.

I am filled with absolute excitement and enthusiasm for you to begin your journey towards designing and living an extraordinary life. My wish is that this book helps you fast-track your journey by providing you with the specific answers you need to get from 'where you are' to 'where you ultimately want to be'!

I look forward to connecting with you and learning how you used this book to create joy, passion, meaning, fulfilment and purpose in your life; to know what worked, and know what didn't work for you.

Connect with me @
www.koonaljain.com
Facebook.com/jain9koonal
Instagram.com/koonaljain_official

I wholeheartedly thank you once again for deciding to take charge of your life and would humbly challenge you not to lose the momentum of this moment. Please jump right into the 'Introduction' where we lay the foundation of this book and carve the way forward.

Remember, you always have a choice.
Choose wisely.

Koonal Jain

P.S.
I have used masculine gender throughout the book only for ease in writing. The philosophies and strategies mentioned apply to all gender identities.

INTRODUCTION

What's the first thought that comes to your mind when you read, 'An Extraordinary Life of Having It All?'

More often than not, the first reaction is usually exhilarating.

However, soon the sceptic inside us takes control and says, 'Stop being so naive, it's too good to be true'.

But why are we so sceptical and pessimistic?

It is because we have been hurt in our past.

Let's face it; we have all had high hopes in the past. And we have all had times when we have failed or when our well-intentioned efforts haven't resulted in the expected favourable outcome.

I do not know what it is that you may have failed at, but I do know that when the outcome wasn't as per your expectation, you would have felt the pain of being disappointed.

Do you remember a time when you saw more darkness than light?

Do you remember a time when you saw more limitations than possibilities?

I certainly do.

It is during those times when our brain develops a survival mechanism wherein we become sceptical and pessimistic as we do not want to go through the same pain again. We are now afraid to get our hopes high as we do not want to look like a fool when we fall flat on the ground.

> *Pessimism: The deadly disease of always looking on the bad side, the problem side, the difficult side, checking all the reasons why it can't be done. The poor pessimist leads an ugly life."*
>
> *—Jim Rohn*

Now, you might say with a heart filled with sarcasm, "Wow, that's such a positive start to a book which is titled The Ultimate Advantage!"

Kindly do not discount me yet.

This **book will definitely provide the recipe for creating the highest possible quality of life that you're capable of living.** But, for you to unleash your full potential and design the life you desire, you must first acknowledge that just because the past didn't turn out the way you wanted, doesn't necessarily mean that your future cannot be better than what you have imagined!

We may have wounds from the past wherein we might have failed a day ago, or a month ago, or may have been failing for the last 6 months, or even in the previous 25 years of our life. But it is of no consequence and makes no difference at all.

All that matters is what you are going to do right now to make sure that your future holds the torch of success high.

Let's not forget, You are not stuck with what you have, you can make it better.

Life is all about cause and effect. You can choose to be the cause of the effect you want.

Now you may be asking yourself, how is this man named Koonal Jain going to help me transform my life around?

I am not going to mince my words here, and I shall be completely honest with you.

The answer to the above question is NOT because I'm a genius.

It's because, over time, I have developed and nurtured a unique skill set which has served me constantly and consistently and has gotten me where I am today.

Today, when I look at my life, I feel blessed to live a life of fulfilment. I am fortunate to be living a life of meaning, a life of joy, a life of passion and a life of purpose where I get to spend every day doing things I genuinely love. On top of that, I'm living my dream where I have the privilege to travel all around the world and stay at the finest of accommodations.

BUT, I wasn't always as blessed or privileged as I am today. I didn't always have this confidence, and I didn't always feel secure. I was lost and had no purpose or meaning in my life.

This ONE skill changed everything. I believe this skill is the key to making the wildest of your dreams a reality!

Now, you may be wondering what that ONE skill is?

It's called **Modelling**.

So what does 'Modelling' even mean?

Modelling is a concept in psychology which states that if you precisely replicate the actions of others, you could reproduce the same quality of results that they had.

Still not clear?

Let me explain.

> *Success leaves clues."*
>
> **—Jim Rohn**

People who have exhibited outstanding excellence and achieved legendary success were able to do so by following a consistent path. You too can experience and achieve the same.

If you can discover and install the mind-set and heart-set of the history makers, if you can adopt the specific strategies and action steps of the game changers, you too can transform and design the life that you desire and deserve.

Now you may say, "Koonal, it's not possible because my problems and circumstances are unique."

Though it may seem like the problem that you're going through in life is unique to you, surprisingly, you are not the first person going through this.

No matter what problem you have right now, someone some-where has had the same problem and figured it out. Whether you have a problem in your business, your relationship, or your career, someone has already faced it and has successfully solved it. It may have taken them decades to solve it, but if you can learn from what they did and apply it to your situation, you can have a solution in a relatively short time.

Simply put, if you are not aware of how to solve a problem, then instead of trying to come up with a brilliant idea yourself, look for someone who's already solved it and apply the same solution to your problem.

There is no surer and shorter way to success than following the footsteps of those who have already achieved it. This is how you can compress decades into days. This is the Ultimate Shortcut to Success.

Please don't get me wrong.

I am in no way sharing this with you to say that I have all the answers or that my life is now flawless. I've had and continue to have my share of testing times. But through it all, I've managed to learn, persist and continue to expand my learning through modelling and consistently work to take my life to the next level.

Modelling is the skill that I have extensively used to establish the foundation and framework of this book.

I've used this skill and obsessively searched for the answer to one elementary question, 'What makes a man or a woman click in life?'

Think about this for a moment:

Why is it that certain individuals who are blessed with all the necessary resources and opportunities to succeed FAIL? While others with seemingly less education, less talent and fewer resources and opportunity SUCCEED?

What motivates people to redefine their life and reach higher levels of success in the first place?

And of those who succeed, why are some miserable while others are fulfilled and live with passion?

Do they know something we don't?

Do they do something we don't?

Is there a science of achievement which we could follow?

Now, you might think this doesn't make sense.

You might think, 'I can't do exactly what Warren Buffet or Mark Zuckerburg did and expect similar results. Times have changed drastically.'

At this point, I must tell you two things.

1. Times may change, but the fundamentals of success and fulfilment will always be the same.
2. The strategies will always need some tweaks.

The way it worked for Warren Buffet might not exactly work for you. But almost always, it will take you 90% of the way. All you need to do then is use your creativity and ingenuity to figure out the last 10% as per your present circumstances.

Now, what seems like a smart choice - figuring out the last 10% or trying to figure out the entire 100%?

The choice seems obvious, doesn't it?

Hence, I went on an odyssey researching and studying heroes who seemed to have it all.

I consciously looked for common patterns among the rare-air and iconic thinkers, leaders, business owners, artists and other heavy-weight champions of their craft.

I then deconstructed their strategies, tools, beliefs, values, actions, behaviours and attitudes. I deconstructed them into simple, actionable steps that we can apply in our life and fast-track our journey towards an extraordinary life of having it all.

By implementing the principles I learned, I was not only able to change the way I felt about my self but also saw a paradigm shift in the results I started producing in my life.

I call the entire process "**The Breadcrumb Trail Protocol**".

The term is borrowed from Hansel and Gretel's fairy-tale where the kids leave a trail of breadcrumbs to trace their way back home. Similarly, we shall use our insight to trace the breadcrumbs along the path used by the game-changers and history-makers and use it to propel our way forward. If we travel in the same direction, we should reach the same destination.

That's where the book comes in.

The book will bring to you the best ideas, strategies, tools, systems, motivation, inspiration, values and beliefs that I've found to be absolutely necessary for peak performance, personal growth, and astounding success. It's been extracted from some of the most successful and influential people in the world.

The information presented in the book shall help you bring about a massive TRANSFORMATION in the way you live by providing a blueprint that enables you to take focused and consistent actions.

Take a moment to ponder, isn't that what you want?

Maybe you want to transform how you feel about yourself (from lack of confidence to developing unshakable belief in yourself and your abilities). Maybe you want extraordinary success in your career or business. Maybe you want more energy or want to become a better communicator. You can create all of these things for yourself and do much more with the effective use of information presented in this book.

To facilitate the same, I have divided the book into 7 Chapters/Training Systems, and I call them '**The 7P's of Ultimate Advantage**' –

1. **P**otential Story,
2. **P**urpose,
3. **P**syche,
4. **P**roductivity,
5. **P**ower state of Peak energy,
6. **P**eople Factor and
7. **P**roof of Concept.

Each chapter looks at a distinct pattern of the 'Breadcrumb Trail of Super-Achievers'. It lays down the specific systems that may assist you in making the biggest leap in the quality of your life. Despite being distinct from each other, all the 7Ps are related, and every chapter builds upon the previous one.

Each of the 7 chapters or 'Training System's stands its ground alone. Yet together, they form the quintessential formula that can be applied to unleash your Ultimate Advantage and create a life you desire and deserve.

Amidst all of it, do you want to know what the best part is?

If you keep reading, you will find out that the power to bring about instantaneous change and turn your dreams into reality is already present within you. You don't have to look outside!

Okay, I know what you might be saying in your head right now, "Koonal, you must be joking. It sounds too good to be true."

I know it does, but I urge you to please not be sceptical and give this a shot.

These 7Ps are proven fundamentals of success that I have extracted after paying very close attention to some of the most extraordinary people in the world. The principles mentioned here have not just worked once, but seem to work almost repeatedly.

I pledge to you that I have poured all my heart, soul and sweat into the book with an obsession to deliver massive value and serve you.

It is my obsession that when you complete this book, you feel you've got a 10X return on your investment in terms of your time and money. This is the level at which I want to play.

But, let me tell you one thing. It takes two to tango!

The book might get you excited with strategies, methodology, models, energy, motivation, and inspiration, but nothing works unless YOU do the work. The real power lies within you.

Think about it.

Is there a difference between 'being excited about something' and 'being committed to it'?

Ofcourse there is. Being excited is a good start, but you certainly need more than excitement to get the good things in life.

You've got to be **Disciplined, Determined, Dedicated** and one more thing that almost everyone considers a taboo word. You have to be **DESPERATE** to get it. That is what I call being in a state of '**D4+**'.

With deep love and respect, I would like to challenge you to be in a state of D4+ (consistently and constantly). Then and only then can YOU truly unleash your Ultimate Advantage and live a truly extraordinary life.

BEWARE: Being in a state of D4+ isn't always easy. However, if you look at the price tag of excellence and success, you will almost always find discomfort and persistence written all over it.

You can choose to take it easy, or you can choose to have an Epic Life. Unfortunately, you cannot have both.

Long story short, 'Living an Extraordinary Life' finally comes down to the quality of your decisions.

So it all adds up to this :

Do you decide to commit to 'D4+' and tap into the power available within you to manifest your dream into reality?

If the answer is 'YES', then it's time to unleash it by jumping onto the next chapter and embracing your ...

ONE

POTENTIAL STORY
The Gateway To Having It All

>   *If we did all the things we are capable of,*
> *we would literally astound ourselves."*
> **—Thomas Edison**

Legend has it, the evil 10 headed Ravana, also known as the 'King of the Demons', fell in love with Sita (wife of Lord Rama), the moment he saw her.

While Lord Rama was away, Ravana abducted her and flew out on his magical chariot holding Sita hostage.

Upon Lord Rama's return, he found his beloved Sita missing. He immediately sent armies of Vanaras (monkeys) in different directions in search of her.

One of these armies was led by Angad, son of Vali, and this team had great heroes like Jambavan and Hanuman. When this team reached the southern tip of the land, they learned that Ravana had imprisoned Sita in Lanka.

To confirm the news, one of the Vanaras had to cross over the ocean to Lanka and verify that Sita was there.

Crossing the sea wasn't an easy task as the length was approximately 1250 kilometres. Suddenly, the entire army of Vanaras was filled with fear and anxiety and contemplated how one could accomplish this task.

The big question was who would be able to make the jump to Lanka?

Team leader Angad tried hard to motivate his army and encouraged someone to volunteer for this herculean task.

Remarkably, Hanuman (someone whose power was beyond anyone's measure) was silent during this entire discussion. He did not offer any opinion or help whatsoever.

Jambavan, the king of bears, also part of Angad's army, knew that Hanuman could jump over the sea with ease. He knew that Hanuman had the potential to kill 1000's of Ravana's soldiers with a single blow of his punch.

Why was Hanuman not stepping up and rising to the occasion? Did he not believe in himself? When Jambavan could see Hanuman's potential, why couldn't Hanuman himself see it?

What was the catch?

Interestingly, as a child, Lord Hanuman was very mischievous (like almost all other babies). On one instance, he flew and literally ate the sun, as he mistook the sun to be a fruit.

One day a powerful sage got angry with Hanuman's naughty behaviour and cursed him to forget about his magical powers (such as the ability to fly or to become infinitely large). The curse would prevail until somebody reminded Hanuman of his powers.

Hence, inspite of having immense potential and being the best in the world he never knew about it. He continued to live under the hypnosis of the curse he was given while he was still a child.

Let's get back to the story of making the jump to Lanka.

At last, Jambavan went up to Hanuman to remind him of his potential and what he could do. Jambavan said:

"You are as powerful as the wind;
You are intelligent, illustrious and an inventor.
There is nothing in this world that's too difficult for you;
Whenever stuck, you are the one who can help."

Finally, Jambawan was able to refresh Hanuman's memory of his powers. Hanuman was able to re-instil positive belief in himself.

Once he regained his belief in himself and his potential, Hanuman crossed India and Lanka's stretch in one leap.

Upon reaching Lanka, he was discovered by Ravana's army, who then set his tail on fire, but he used that very fire to burn down Lanka.

Later, Hanuman also flew to the Himalayas and returned with a mountain full of medicinal herbs to restore the wounded in Lord Rama's army.

If you asked Lord Rama, he would vouch for Hanuman being the single most crucial warrior in his war against Ravana.

Think about this for a moment.

Someone like Hanuman, who had extraordinary superhuman potential, couldn't do anything until he was consciously aware of it.

You may be wondering why am I telling you this story about Hanuman?

Here's why.

Is there even a slight possibility that like Hanuman, you too are living in a hypnotic trance and are not aware of your true potential?

Think about this for a moment - *What if you are the absolute best at something, and you don't know about it yet?*

What if you have infinite potential and gifts and you still haven't harnessed them yet?

Is that a possibility?

Ask yourself, *would you have lived your life differently, if you knew with absolute certainty and belief, that you had the potential within you to be the absolute best at something?*

Now, you might say "Koonal, I have never really thought about it!"

Sometimes, I find it really amusing that we know so little about our own self, and because we are so busy, somehow surviving our life and making ends meet, we continue to live in this ignorant state of not knowing the very essence of who we really are!

Most of us spend a fair amount of our living years getting a formal education, where we learn all sorts of things. Still, we never end up learning the answer to a basic fundamental question, "WHO AM I?".

To solve the mystery, I decided it would be best to research and take reference from two of the most reliable sources known to humanity –

1. Theology (religious beliefs and theory when developed systematically)
2. Science.

So, here it goes.

As per theology, God is the source of everything that exists in this world. Everything we see around us emanates/originates from God's energy. Therefore, human beings are also part and parcel of God's energy.

Also, as per theology, God possesses infinite potential including all knowledge, all strength, all fame, all beauty and all riches.

Here's where it gets interesting...

A small particle of gold also has all the qualities of gold; a drop of water from the ocean is also salty. Similarly, both you and I, being part and parcel of God, have all the qualities of God, including infinite potential within us.

Here's the best part, God is equally present in both you and I as he was in Einstein and Edison. On that account, we have the same talent and ability as the extraordinary legends like Einstein and Edison. What we do with our skill and ability is entirely up to us.

> 66 *God's gift to you is more talent and ability that you will ever use in your lifetime,*
> *Your gift to God is to develop as much of talent and ability as you can, in this lifetime."*
>   — **Steve Bow**

Let me guess; you're still not convinced about the infinite potential available within you?

Please stay with me as there's more to it.

You might be wondering, what's next?

Keep reading, and you'll find out what the realm of science has to say regarding "Who am I?".

Let's get things clear - modern science doesn't believe in the concept of the soul beyond the body.

Science believes that the human body is a combination of physical elements and that life comes into existence when the physical elements combine with certain chemical elements under a specific environmental condition.

The interaction of different elements led to evolution, giving rise to more than 8.7 million species on earth.

We should be incredibly proud of the fact that out of the 8.7 million species, you and I are the most evolved. We possess a central nervous system that will make even the most complex supercomputer look like a toy!

It has been proved empirically that our brains have more than 100,000,000,000 (100 billion) neurons, 2 million support cells capable of 10,000 operations per second.

In short, almost all brains have genius ability and infinite potential. Be it Einstein, be it Edison or be it you and I, we are all blessed with similar hardware.

I get it; I get it...

If almost all brains have the ability to be genius, then why aren't all of us geniuses?

Let me explain.

Of all the species, it is commonly stated that humans are the only ones who CAN use 10% of the brain's capacity. (Fun fact: Only dolphins can use their brains more than us, i.e., 20% of their brains capacity).

10% might seem less, but if you look around, you would appreciate the marvels that we've accomplished using just 10% capacity of our brain.

Now, to answer the pertaining question, why aren't we all geniuses?

Ironically, there's a big difference between CAN use 10% and using 10% of the brain's capacity.

Most of us do not spend enough time, energy, or resources in developing our neurons (neural pathways) that may enable us to use 10% of our brain capacity.

When it comes to using 10% capacity of the brain, we can safely say: Anyone can use it, but not everyone will use it. Fair enough?

Here's the scary part.

No matter which branch of logic you choose (theology or science), you will have to accept the ultimate truth of you having deep reservoirs of infinite potential available within yourself.

Whether you choose to unleash the same or not is a different story altogether.

Good news is: We are all-powerful, unique and wonderful. Let's never doubt that! We can find our way to anything we want.

But hang on a minute! *If we have infinite potential, then why don't our results always reflect our potential?*

It's because of the 'Potential Story' we keep telling ourselves.

Believe it or not, we are all EXPERTS at story-telling!

Almost all of us have big DREAMS and ASPIRATIONS, but we keep telling ourselves –

I'm too old
I'm too young
I am not lucky
I don't have the time
I don't have the experience
I don't have the resources
I don't have the degree
I don't have the network/connections
I don't have the money.

The above narratives are stories that hold us back from tapping into our true potential and design the extraordinary life of having it all.

Simply put, Potential Story is a set of mental rules and assumptions on how we perceive our potential. It's what we believe to be the absolute truth (whether or not it is)!

The potential story is our beliefs about what is possible and what is not possible. It's our belief about what we can do and what we cannot do, also our beliefs about what can happen and about what cannot happen.

How often have you caught yourself saying "I would like to do this/have this but I cannot because...?

Whatever follows "because" is your Negative Potential Story.

So, What's your Potential Story?

What do you keep telling yourself that stops you from achieving your dreams?

Ask yourself, how do you see yourself in the story of life? Do you see yourself as a winner, or do you see yourself as someone who is always a step behind everyone else?

By the way, do you know what the worst part is?

If you keep telling yourself the same stories repeatedly, you get caught up in a hypnotic trance where you start believing them to be absolutely true. You end up becoming an extra in your own movie!

Our story and belief about our potential can dictate the direction of our lives, for better or for worse, and if you think about it, they apparently come out of nowhere.

Although they must come from somewhere, right?

So, where do our potential stories come from, and why do we start believing and living in the hypnotic trance of our negative potential story?

HYPNOTIC TRANCE OF MEDIOCRITY
You are Born Perfect, Programmed into Mediocre.

BELIEF FUNNEL

(What You Think You Can Do)

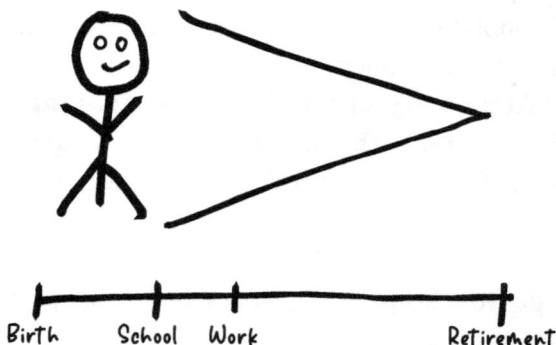

Birth   School   Work   Retirement

POTENTIAL FUNNEL

(What You Can Actually Do)

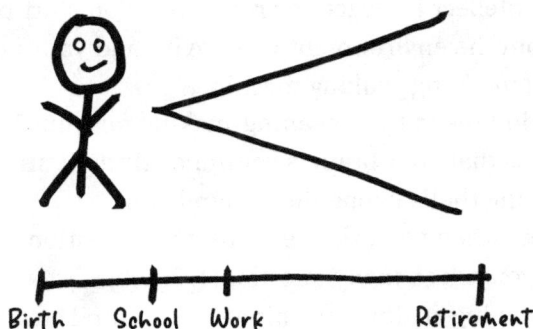

Birth   School   Work   Retirement

More often than not, potential stories are developed as a child (similar to mighty Hanuman) and stick with you like glue into adulthood.

You see, when you are born, you are born with the gift of infinite potential. As a child, you are connected to your greatest self and your most authentic nature. You are connected to your gifts, your talents and your abilities.

As a child, you have no conscious fear. You dare to dream big. You dare to have heroic ambitions and to take risks. You have energy and spunk. You speak the truth. You radiate positivity and possibility of being able to do anything!

Then again, you are also innocent. You express freely without thinking what others will say. You are proud to be in the full expression of who you truly are!

As a child, you keep asking questions: Why does this happen? Why does that happen? You are curious.

And here's the sad part. This is where you are tricked! This is where the world puts a veil over your eyes.

You get adulterated by loving and well-intentioned adults, by the environment, by society.

They take advantage of you being innocent and suck you into their world of Mediocrity!

Kindly Note: As a child, your mind is wide open. You do not have the intellect to negate or reject yet. You start picking up things from the environment you are in, and your brain operates like a meaning-making machine.

What do I mean by a meaning-making machine?

It means that your brain is continuously assigning meaning to everything that's happening around you.

You see, when you ask questions, they question you back – "Why do you ask so many questions!?"

The meaning-making machine in your mind starts processing the information and starts giving meaning to it.

You now start believing, 'Asking questions is not good', and you accept what they say.

When you cry in public, they say – "Don't cry too loud".

And when you get angry in front of people, they say, "Don't throw tantrums in front of others".

You now start believing you shouldn't express freely. It's okay to suppress hurt, pain, anger and sadness (which sadly leads to depression later.)

What's more, they promise you something, and they break it or lie to you. You now start believing it's okay to lie, it's okay to not keep up to your commitment.

When you're playing and testing your capabilities, lovingly, they say, "Be careful, don't you fall, you'll hurt yourself". You now start believing it's not good to take risks, and this is how you learn to be fearful.

In school, when you daydream about the possibility of the things you could do, the teacher would tell you, "Will you stop what you're doing/thinking and pay more attention here?"

When you dare to do something out of the box, your friends and family laugh at you, mock you and question you "Who do you think you are?"

This is how you start losing sight of your greatest self.

What's more?

You see almost everyone working all the time, running after money and being stressed and worried. You see them not enjoying the work they do. You see them dreaming small but wanting more.

You look at them, and your meaning-making machine starts installing beliefs, values, habits and starts accepting that this is how one should live.

You tend to accept whatever you see, whatever you hear, whatever you eat, whatever you are told - without ever questioning.

The messaging around you starts to form your programming!

This is how you learn the language you speak. This is how you learn to like the food you eat. This is why you wear the clothes you wear. This is how you accept the name they call you by.

Simply stated, just as a disease spreads from host to victim, beliefs also end up spreading in a similar way.

We often take on information and believe them to be true, not based on logic or rationale, but rather through Social Contagion. Social Contagion is a natural tendency for a person to copy a specific behaviour of others who are either in the vicinity or whom they have been exposed to.

All in all, society teaches you how to think. They teach you how to operate. They tell you who you need to be.

As most of them you see live a life of Mediocrity, they seduce you into believing you too are meant to live a life of Mediocrity!

Have you ever heard someone around you say "That's just my luck" or "I'm not gifted enough"? Or have you heard them blaming others or justifying and giving excuses when something terrible happens?

I bet you have!

This is how your potential story gets shaped as you start picking up these false beliefs and stories from the world around you. That's how you start living in their hypnotic trance.

Stephen R. Covey presented it beautifully when he said, "We see the world, not as it is, but as we are - or, as we are conditioned to see it."

Be warned; you do not see the world as the world is, you see the world through your own lenses, which is coloured by the filters of your perception.

Your perception is shaped by the information you have consumed, by all the experiences you've had and the meanings you have associated with them. These have formed your belief system, which now becomes your version of the truth.

Our potential story is our own version of beliefs, which we believe to be completely true, and as we believe them to be true, they become our truth. They become the reality of our world.

Can you now see a pattern in why you do what you do, and why you think what you think? You have been programmed into thinking and believing into this.

But how important is a potential story?

You may look at a potential story like an operating system of a computer.

Just like an operating system has total control over how a computer functions, your potential story has almost exclusive control over the way you think, the way you behave, your values, habits, daily choices, and the way you act with your body.

Ultimately, it controls the way you live your life - your creativity, your productivity, your energy, your income, your lifestyle, and your impact on people around you.

Now, the question is, is your existing potential story helping you?

If your potential story is negative (filled with limiting beliefs), you end up being stuck and stifled. You will never be able to make any progress in life beyond a certain point, and life will be very limiting.

On the other hand, if your potential story is positive, it will make you have a positive outlook towards life. You will have a limitless self-image which would enable you to live an extraordinary life. It will empower you to adapt to upsets and unforeseen life events easily.

Let me share a small incident with you.

In December 2016, I had to take a flight from New Delhi to Kolkata (my hometown) at around 6 A.M. I called for an Uber to go from the hotel to the airport. I was running late to reach the airport.

It was 4 A.M., and the roads were relatively empty, but still, my uber driver was driving at a constant speed of 80 km/hour.

As I was running late, I asked my uber driver, "Sir, why don't you accelerate as the roads have very few cars and traffic is negligible?"

What he said next, was astonishing for me.

He told me that the car couldn't go above 80 km/hour even if he wanted to, as there was a 'speed governor' in the car. I didn't know what a speed governor was, so I asked him to clarify it.

He clarified that in an attempt to tackle the increasing number of accidents, the State Government had installed speed governors on buses, trucks, small commercial vehicles and taxis.

It is a device whose primary function is to control and regulate the vehicle's speed and not let it exceed the pre-specified value. And it was 80km/hour in the Uber's case.

Oddly enough, even though the car can easily hit 120 to 130 km/hr on an empty road, it now won't exceed 80 km/hour. It doesn't even matter how hard you step on the accelerator. All the extra horsepower in the car is idle, and it cannot run at its full potential.

You may wonder why am I telling you this?

Here's the real deal!

The point I am trying to drive home is that our potential story is similar to a speed governor installed in a car. A Negative Potential story will ensure that you keep operating at 80 km/hour even though there is infinite horsepower available within you!

Similar to the speed governor, the negative potential story does not allow any acceleration in our life. This speed governor is controlled by all the limiting beliefs, habits, values and morals that we have formed during our existence.

No matter how hard you push the accelerator, the potential story won't let you use the extra horsepower available within you. After a few failed attempts, you will give up and not even try anymore.

So the bottom line is this: to unleash your true potential, you will first have to remove your speed governor, i.e. the negative and limiting potential story.

But before you can consciously remove them, you must first be able to differentiate between what I call: Negotiable and Non-Negotiable truth!

NON-NEGOTIABLE TRUTH AND NEGOTIABLE TRUTH

66 *If you would be a real seeker after truth, it is neces-sary that at least once in your life you doubt, as far as possible, all things."*

— **René Descartes**

You must be wondering; truth is truth. How can we bifur-cate truth into Non-negotiable truth and Negotiable truth!

But just keep reading, and I'll explain.

So, What's a Non-negotiable truth?

Non-negotiable truth exist in the realm of the physical world. They are based on facts. And all of us are likely to agree on the same. We can either touch it, feel it or prove it.

Examples of Non-Negotiable truth are – fire is hot, water is wet, gravity keeps pulling us back and keeps us on the ground. You can't negotiate or doubt the authenticity of it.

What's a Negotiable truth then?

Negotiable truth is something that exists in the realm of the mental world.

Negotiable truth are usually based on opinion and agreement (and not on facts). These are ideas, beliefs, concepts, and rules that living beings have developed and passed on through generations.

Examples of Negotiable truth are – ideas about religion, ideas about marriage, ideas about love and loyalty, ideas and laws about borders and nations, ideas about right education, ideas about our potential and talents. They also include opinions about money, luck, hard work etc.

Here is something exciting!

Have you ever seen an actual border that divides nations?

I haven't.

If you search for an actual border that divides nations, you would be utterly disappointed not to find any. Not even a faint line. Yet so many of us feel connected to our country and are willing to give our lives for the same. This is because, in our mental world, we accept the border to be true!

How about the institution of marriage?

Every culture has its own views about marriage. Some cultures permit only one marriage at a time while others permit more than one. There is no scientific way of proving which way is the only correct way. But we tend to accept whatever our culture decides for us.

Steve Jobs said, "Life can be so much broader, once you discover one simple fact, and that is that everything around you that you call 'life' was made up by people who were no smarter than you. And you can change it, you can influence it, you can build your own things that other people can use."

The rules of society that define how we should live, how we should dress, how we should behave and think, and how we should define success and failure are mere guidelines for living that have been accepted by cultures.

These are certainly not proven facts or non-negotiable truths!

Then again, we consider them as truth and never question their authenticity because they are embedded deep within us since childhood. By hearing the same thing over and over again, we start accepting it as the truth.

So, what's the point here?

My point is this – As long as you get faith and power to have an empowering potential story from the negotiable truth, it is acceptable.

But when negotiable truths start forcing you into living a life that is limited, you can negotiate your way out of it. You can free yourself from what society has hypnotised you into believing who you are.

Once you understand that the rules or beliefs about your potential story aren't completely true, you might still have to play the game within the rules of the world, but you can at least choose to play your own game. (Obviously, the caveat here is that you do not hurt others in the process.)

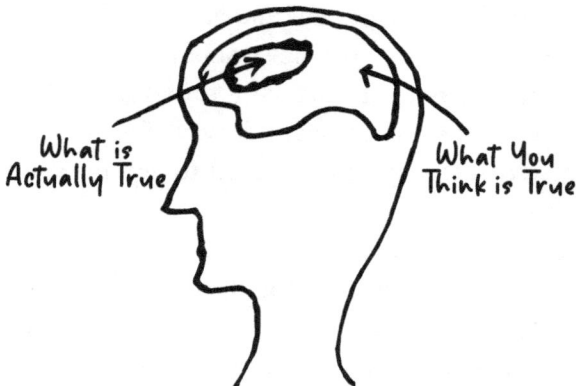

What is Actually True

What You Think is True

Below are some of the most common negotiable truths that limit us from unleashing and living our true potential.

By acknowledging and changing them, you will be able to create the opportunities for success and fulfilment that will help you create an extraordinary life.

Let's get started!

1. They Can, But I can't syndrome

> *Right here we come to a rather strange fact. We tend to minimise the things we can do, the goals we can accomplish, and for some equally strange reason we think other people can do things that we cannot."*
>
> **— Earl Nightingale**

Does this sound familiar?

Have you ever seen someone extraordinarily talented and admired them? Someone iconic, someone world-class, someone legendary who was too good to be true?

It could be a sportsperson, an entrepreneur, a scientist, a speaker, a painter, an actor, a musician or anyone else.

Have you ever been mesmerised by their achievements or their magical ability to execute flawlessly and with incredible finesse? Looking at them you said to yourself "they are so lucky that they are gifted; I wish I could do it too!"

I certainly have!

I somehow convinced myself that they are different, that they are lucky. I convinced myself that they are gifted and can do things against the grain because they are constructed from a different fabric of cloth.

But why do we think they are gifted?

It is natural to think so because when we see them, we see them in their full glory.

What we don't see is the struggle they had to go through.

What we don't see is the level of commitment and discipline they had.

What we don't see is the 'I won't give up till I reach my dream' attitude.

What we don't see is the time, energy, resources they put in towards improving their craft day in and day out.

You know what, almost every genius has the same backstory.

Every genius is nothing but a full expression of their potential, nurtured through deliberate practice. They are not born genius. They persist till they achieve genius.

Ever heard of the 10000 hours rule?

Anders K Ericsson, a Swedish Psychologist, who is internationally recognised as a researcher on peak human performance, proves that it takes 10000 hours (on an average) of deliberate practice to be world-class at anything.

It's important to note here that Anders K. Ericsson uses the word "deliberate practice" and not just "practice".

What's the difference between the two?

Practice means gaining experience by spending more hours doing the same thing.

However, deliberate practice is an art.

Deliberate practice states that you continuously set goals that are slightly higher than what you can currently do, and then stretch your ability to achieve them. It's a form of practice where you pinpoint specific areas of improvement and then practice to excel.

When done regularly, you start getting better at it, and, after 10000 hours of deliberate practice, you become an expert.

Therefore, we can say that the genius or world-class performers did have some natural talent, but they had to put in 10000 hours of deliberate practice on a particular skill to be labelled as a legend.

Deliberate practice is the real gamechanger.

Kindly remember: It was not a revelation but a long journey!

What's the point syndrome –
The only thing that's stopping you!!

Anyone can become a world-class legend at something, but not everyone will become.

Most of us don't even try to become a legend because we believe that legends are gifted and that we aren't.

This misconception makes us feel that we aren't worthy of becoming a legend, and we do not hone our skills. We do not invest the time, energy, resources, discipline, habits and rituals, and the 10000 hours of deliberate practice required to be a legend.

We tell ourselves "what's the point" in working so hard since we will never be a legend. We convince ourselves that it's going to be a waste of time even to try!

Guess what happens next? You end up not being a legend. You keep playing the small game.

It's a vicious circle.

The game would change if we believe and have faith in ourselves and our infinite potential.

If we believe with certainty and conviction, that we can be the best at something, we will then do the work required to be a legend.

Guess what will happen when you put in the 10000 hours of deliberate practice at whatever you do?

You will be an expert and world-class level at it! This is what some people call the "Self-Fulfilling Prophecy".

And Boom! From vicious, it now becomes a virtuous circle.

No wonder, every religious book on the planet, talks about the power of belief or faith. That's because it's the law that governs how your brain works.

In short, it all adds up to this: Your belief about your potential will decide whether you will be able to live your potential or not.

Someone will be the next Bill Gates.

Someone will be the next Zuckerberg.

Someone will be the next Nelson Mandela.

Someone will be the next Narendra Modi.

Someone will be the next Sachin Tendulkar.

Why can't that someone be you?

We have already proved that you have infinite potential.

Are you willing to put in the 10000 hours of deliberate practice required to go through the journey and unleash the genius within you?

The choice is yours.

Rather than having a negative potential story (they can and I can't), we can choose an empowering alternative where we feel, **'I can and I will. I believe in myself. I believe I can get whatever I want. I am willing to do whatever it takes. I am unstoppable!'**

> 66 *Think you can, think you can't;*
> *either way you'll be right."*
>
> **–Henry Ford**

2. Luck is everything

One of the most common limiting beliefs is that we have no control over our fate and that luck is everything. This is by far one of the most destructive beliefs in our potential story that limits us from getting the success that we desire and living the life we deserve.

To begin with, this is somewhat true. We cannot control most of the things that happen to us.

Think about it...

Did you have any control over who your parents would be or what day, time and month would you be born?

Did you have any control on whether you would be born in a family that has access to ultimate luxury or to a family that's barely surviving?

Did you have control on how tall you would be or what your skin colour would be?

I guess not.

Also, we cannot control the pull of gravity. We cannot control whether the world would be in a state of recession or a boom, war or peace!

That being the case, it is natural for us to feel that we have absolutely no control over our fate and someone else is in control of what we see, feel and do!

"Luck is everything" gives us a feeling of being powerless and victimised.

Most people living on the planet have this belief and play victim by:

1. Blaming (It's not my fault – it's the fault of my parents/government/anyone else but not me!)
2. Complaining (Why me? What wrong did I do to go through this?)
3. Justifying (It was meant to happen this way)

Ask yourself, have you ever blamed, justified or complained about your circumstances or someone else for your misery?

I certainly have!

But you know what, extraordinary individuals accept the circumstance (instead of blaming, justifying and complaining) and respond to it. They not only get through difficult times, but they somehow find an opportunity to improve their lives and the lives of people around them. They use these challenges to fuel their growth from ordinary to extraordinary.

How do they do it?

George Bernard Shaw summarised it beautifully. He said, "People are always blaming their circumstances for what they are. I don't believe in circumstances. The people who get on in this world are the people who get up and look for the circumstances they want, and if they can't find them, make them."

They successfully change their potential story from 'Luck is everything' to an empowering story where they believe they are in charge. They will either find the way or make their way.

Extraordinary people understand they can't control the rain. They accept it and choose to either carry an umbrella or wear a raincoat, and some even take it one step further. They start collecting the rainwater and use it to their advantage.

Take a moment to ponder if you have ever come across or heard about someone who had to go through a tragedy? For whom life had been seemingly unfair. They have had to go through stress caused by mental, emotional and physical abuse. But they refused to give up.

They chose not to blame, justify, or complain about their circumstances. They came out of that adversity as a winner, and they ended up making a dent in the universe. These are the Mahatma Gandhi's, Nelson Mandela's, and Oprah Winfrey's who shift cultures.

They became extraordinary by taking full responsibility of their circumstances and felt they were in control of their actions and masters of their fate. They took effective decisions based on the choices available to them. They defied luck by demonstrating that life happens for them and through them.

There are examples galore.

An untrained novice eye will see that as luck. But that's not the case.

Once you study their backstory, you will realise it was a result of preparation, persistence and endurance of pain.

This is where people create reality with their thoughts, actions and persistence. This is where real growth takes place. This is where you start manifesting and bending reality and start finding new ways to play in the world.

This is where you start to leave behind most of the people who are living a life that's ordinary and start curating a life that's truly extraordinary. These are the people who get on in this world!

To sum up, rather than having a victim mindset 'that life happens to us', we can choose an empowering alternative where we feel that:

- **The world doesn't happen to me! Sure, I can't always control things, but by taking action and moving towards what I want, I make my way and attract the positive things in the universe.**
- **I am responsible for my world. I create my world. I am the master of my fate, and I can make my destiny.**

3. I am not enough – The termite that makes you hollow from inside!

Have you ever come across or heard about someone who has everything in life, everything one could dream of, and still isn't very happy and wants more and more?

Surprisingly, they have a feeling that they aren't wealthy enough!

Let me ask you something else...

Have you ever wanted to say something at work or to someone you respect, but you did not say it because a little voice in your head questioned you "What If I am wrong?" or "What if they don't like what I say and start judging me?"

And you didn't end up saying it because (probably) you had a feeling that you weren't smart or interesting enough!

Though the above two questions may seem completely unrelated, the underlying reason for both the above feelings is the same.

It's a feeling of "I am not enough"!

It's a limiting belief of self-doubt that either stops you from taking action or it makes you go overboard to prove something to the world!

You always evaluate yourself and feel that somehow you should (1) be more and (2) do more. It is because internally you don't feel worthy, you feel – 'I am not enough'!

Scientific studies and research have proved time and again that the common denominator of almost all our emotional issues arises from believing that we are not enough.

We are continually feeling we are not smart enough, not successful enough, not interesting enough, not attractive enough, not wealthy enough, and most of all, not lovable enough.

I was curious. How does this message of "I am not enough" get internalised? Where does this belief come from?

Marissa Peer, Britain's #1 Therapist, who has been associated with the world's top performers and elite such as rock stars, CEO's, Olympic athletes, royalty and Oscar-winning actors, states that within each of us is a child who never received the love, appreciation and attention they deserved.

Marissa Peer went on to further confirm that if you study some of the most beautiful, talented and admired people in the world, including the likes of Amy Winehouse, Heath Ledger, Robin Williams, Whitney Houston, George Michael, Michael Jackson, Princess Diana, you would realise that, not one of those people ever believed they were enough.

They were talented, beautiful, gifted, extraordinary, got more wealth than most could dream of. Millions admired them, and still, almost all of them got treated for different drug addiction, alcoholism, bulimia, or depression. They were never satiated and wanted more because deep down they felt they were not enough.

If you analyse, you would realise that she is correct.

No matter how much you love your child, no matter how hard you try, you will have to, at some point of time tell your child negative statements with words that include "No", "Stop", "Don't", "Can't" etc.

Even loving parents who know about child psychology will have to do it, let alone parents who are not aware of the harm they are doing to their kids.

As discussed earlier, the meaning-making machine in a child's brain keeps giving meaning to every negative statement they come across. It starts forming a belief that I am not enough.

Picture this...

If a child doesn't eat food, they are told, "Eat, or I shall not talk to you".

The child now starts believing that love is conditional. And mom/dad will only love me if I do this particular activity. I am not lovable enough. Then a child would sometimes end up eating to prove that they are worthy of being loved.

To get love, they are made to prove a point or validate it!

There's more...

As a child, if they pick up something valuable that's fragile, they are told: "Don't do it, or you may break it". The child starts believing, "Mom and dad don't trust me as I am not responsible enough".

As a child, they would learn something or discover something new, and they would run excitedly to their parents to share the same.

Parents being parents, might be busy over a seemingly important phone call, or a regular chore and might end up saying "Please show it to me later" or "Can't you see, I am busy". The child starts believing, "I am not interesting enough".

In spite of knowing the same, I am guilty of doing it.

Adolescence and adulthood come with different challenges. Now, the meaning-making machine starts validating and internalising the feeling of "I am not enough".

Your first crush doesn't like you back – You feel, "I am not lovable enough".

Your date doesn't call you back – You feel, "I am not interesting enough".

Your grades were not perfect in Math or science or any other subject – You feel, "I am not smart or intelligent enough".

Your friends bully you and say horrible things for the way you look (acne, height, skin colour, hair etc.) – You feel, "I am not good looking enough".

You didn't get the dream job or didn't earn as much you wanted to – You feel, "I am not deserving enough".

The meaning-making machines keep confirming that "I am not enough"!

We don't express this feeling as society doesn't appreciate showing negative emotions. Now, the emotion that has been repressed and suppressed doesn't just die out.

Emotions are energy, which is always there. The energy is still in you, but it got subsided by the other things that happen in your life.

Now you want to, and end up doing things not to be happy, but to prove to others and validate that you are enough!

We pursue fame and chase money because we somehow think that once we have it, we will prove to the world that "I am enough".

But it just doesn't work, because no matter what you do, the scar remains. You are only treating the symptoms and not the disease.

As the scar is still there, we keep serving the world with angst, frustration, guilt, anxiety and depression within us.

On that account, it becomes vital to reactivate the feeling of "I am enough". Otherwise, no matter how your life turns out, you will keep wanting more and keep on doing more and more, not to be happy but to prove something to the world.

At this point, you must realise, it's a journey that's never-ending and a dead-end at the same time. The only way out is to change your self-image (the image of your own worth).

Think about it...

Have you been in an argument or seen someone in an argument?

The worst part about being in an argument is that after a point, people end up forgetting what the argument was all about. It soon becomes all about winning.

We hate when someone proves us wrong and dismisses our opinion/idea because we feel that dismissal of our opinion/ideas is a dismissal of our own self.

We cannot take criticism because we suffer from low self-esteem, and we turn hostile towards the person who criticised us.

It's all because of the scar deep inside us which is trying to prove or validate that we are enough.

The game changes once we get to the root of the problem and start fixing the scar of "I am not enough". The game changes when we start living, breathing, walking, talking, behaving and believing the fact that we are enough.

It is not merely knowing but believing with unwavering certainty and unshakable conviction that "I am enough".

Nobody can minimise you or diminish you by criticising you when you know that you're enough and that you do not require any validation from anyone. You then stop arguing unnecessarily, and you start accepting criticism constructively.

Legends like Edison, Einstein, and Mandela (to name a few) had internalised the belief that they are enough.

They never ran endlessly after fame and money (to prove a point) nor did they seek any validation from the people around them.

They experienced the world in a whole new light. They were motivated by their inner happiness and seemed to care two hoots about criticism or praise.

Ask yourself, have you designed your life in a way, wherein you live to please others?

If yes, then rather than having a negative potential story that "I am not enough", we can choose an empowering potential story where we feel that:

"I am good enough. I am smart and lovable. I am worthy of making conversation with anyone as I am interesting enough. Knowing that I am good enough makes me feel confident and comfortable. It keeps me motivated to do things that make me happy"!

'I AM ENOUGH' PARADOX!

I know what you feel. You feel overwhelmed by the above idea but also confused.

Isn't the desire to get praise (external validation) the driving force for us to have big dreams and do big things in the world? Wouldn't knowing the fact that "I am enough" make us lazy and seek pleasure without working hard?

Marissa Peer, the expert psychologist whom we mentioned before, has answered this beautifully. From her extensive research and work with the who's who and VIPs of the world she has been able to satisfactorily prove that:

The desire to get praise may be a driving force for you to have big dreams and motivate you to go for it, but, that's not the optimal path. It requires you to pay a hefty price – the price of letting go of happiness in your quest for greatness.

You may end up chasing money and fame to impress others, might even end up getting it, and later realise that, it doesn't satisfy or satiate you. You end up always wanting more and more, unable to enjoy what you already have. It's a hollow victory.

On the contrary, it might seem that a person who feels that he is enough might end up being a satisfied couch potato. By contrast, nothing could be further from the truth.

No matter how successful you are, you haven't unleashed your true potential, your self-actualised greatest self, unless you believe you are enough. You're living in constant pain (the pain of potential unexpressed).

When you think you're not enough, you play SAFE. You don't try to stretch beyond your comfort zone because you fear failure, rejection and what others will think about you.

You fear your inner insecurities; you fear that if you fail, the world will come to know that you're indeed not enough.

Only when you feel that you're enough, you will take uninhibited and relentless action. That's when you go all out to realise your self-actualised greatest self. You follow your heart's true desire without wondering what the world will think.

You go all out because now you understand that if you fail, it's not because of you (as you know you're enough). It's probably because of the methods or skills or approach or whatever (but not you). That being the case, you don't quit and keep changing your approach. You keep upgrading your skills and trying until you succeed to be the most excellent version of yourself.

Long story short, knowing you are enough is a positive potential story that gives you the unshakable courage to be Unfuckwithable and Do your Best!

*Unfuckwithable meaning: (adj.) when you're truly at
peace and in touch with yourself, and nothing anyone says
or does bother you, and no negativity or external drama can
touch you.*

LIFE RE-ENGINEERING –
DEATH BY DESIGN

The biggest act of infidelity is to cheat your greatest self! It's
the greatest sin!

Let us start the journey to re-engineer our lives and reclaim
our greatest self. Let us change our potential story to light up
the valley of darkness and access the deep reservoirs of infinite
potential within us.

To be able to reclaim our true heroic nature and infinite potential, we must:

1. be willing to remove our limiting beliefs and
2. be able to upgrade our potential story with empowering
   beliefs.

Before we proceed, may I ask you, are you prepared for a
war!?

The potential story is deeply rooted within us, and as discussed earlier, they have almost exclusive control over you.

Any attempt you make to alter your potential story will disrupt and frighten you. It will make you challenge everything
you have ever lived on: the very essence of your identity might
shake up!

The beliefs will not give up easily and keep coming back to
you. They will resist, fight back and trick your mind into being
a hostage again.

Hence, to be able to have long-lasting change and to improve
our life, we need to start a war. A committed, disciplined and

persistent war to kill the negative potential stories which are nothing but limiting beliefs that are not true.

Each time we kill our limiting belief, a little part of us dies with it. Each time we upgrade our potential story with empowering beliefs, we rise like a phoenix to unleash our ultimate advantage.

We will not leave it to chance anymore; we will deliberately design the death of our negative potential story. It will be death by design.

But what weapon will we use to kill our negative potential story?

The answer lies in one word— REPETITION!

Now you might wonder how repetition can help you?

I would like to take you on a journey way back in time.

Now, go as far back as you can. Go back to the time when you were an infant. When you were just born, and you had no name.

An undeniable fun fact: You did not choose your name. Your parents chose a name for you.

Now, let's start playing forward the scenes in your mind.

Imagine, the first time your mother calls out your name.

Do you think you would have reacted to that word?

Probably not. It's just a random word for you. You don't relate to it.

Imagine, the second time your mother calls out your name.

Do you think you would have reacted to that word now?

Probably not even now.

Third. Fourth. Fifth. Sixth time she calls your name – I would guess the reaction would pretty much be the same – NO REACTION. It's just a random word for you.

You get the point, right?

She keeps on repeating your name until one day when you start getting curious. You think to yourself, "Is she calling out to me?". You look at her, and it seems like she is indeed calling out to you.

You're still not sure, but you start getting a feeling that MAYBE you're supposed to react to that word. Your meaning-making machine in the brain starts looking for meaning in that word.

Now the feeling starts getting reaffirmed and internalised.

Every time she repeats your name, you realise she is calling out to you. Now, your meaning-making machine starts giving meaning to that word. You start believing it's an important word and you should react to it.

Then it starts to hit you. The repetition of that word, again and again, makes your brain believe that it indeed is your name. It starts etching it in your subconscious mind. More repetition of the same word, it changes from being just a random word to your identity.

This is the power of repetition.

It has the power to make you believe that one word, which was once a random word to you, is now your identity. It makes you believe YOU ARE YOUR NAME!

Had your parents chosen a different word as your name, and repeated it often enough, you would have believed it to be true as well.

Repetition is the most potent weapon in your arsenal!

We will now use the same weapon to hack your subconscious mind into believing whatever we want.

Here's how we will do it.

We will repeat the same empowering beliefs with corresponding emotions over and over again until we start believing them to be absolutely true.

What do you think will happen if you consistently and constantly repeat empowering beliefs with corresponding emotion? The positive belief will superimpose themselves and collapse the old negative belief structures that don't belong there.

In a nutshell, repeatedly speak what you wish to become! Only Speak what causes you to feel, experience and be your best.

Now you know why, don't you?

Because what you consistently speak with the emotional intensity - you will believe, you will experience, and you will create. The words that you speak with enough emotional conviction will drive and dictate the direction of your life.

*Kindly visit www.theultimateadvantage.club and download a power-packed list of empowering beliefs that help you in cultivating a **NO MATTER WHAT** attitude.*

RED PILL OR BLUE PILL: YOU CHOOSE!

The key takeaway from this chapter is that our Potential Story determines whether we will do the work required to live our potential or not.

Now, it's time to make a choice!

In the movie, The Matrix, the leader Morpheus offers the main character Neo a choice between a red pill and a blue pill.

The blue pill represents living in a beautiful prison. It would mean living a life of ignorance (of his real powers). Living an average, mediocre life where you are blinded by the routine box you live your life in - quite similar to the life most people live now.

The red pill represents true freedom from the enslaving

control of the machine-generated dream world (limiting potential story in our case). This truth of reality will help him unleash his true potential, but it would be more difficult than the beautiful prison. Similar to the situation where we reclaim our heroic self to live an extraordinary and fulfilled life.

Now I would like to flip the same question to you.

Which pill do you choose?

Red or Blue?

If you choose the blue pill and would want to live with the same limiting potential story, I would humbly request you with folded hands to not read this book further. It will be a mere waste of time.

However, if you decide to choose the red pill, and are willing to play full out and design the life you desire and deserve, then continue onto the next chapter where we will start curating the life of your dreams and discover your life's true...

TWO

PURPOSE
The Currency Of Passion

  Life is either a daring adventure or nothing at all!"

                   –Hellen Keller

Have you ever wondered why you get out of bed every day? You are bound to think that's such a redundant and silly question!

You might say, "The reason I get out of bed is the same reason everybody gets out of bed", and the reason most of us get out of bed is to get to work so that we can earn money.

As discussed earlier, we pick up ways of living life from people around us without ever questioning; and because almost everyone in the world is living like this, we start to believe this is how one should live.

That being the case, most of us have no clue why we're doing what we're doing!

We take the liberty to assume that, if most people are doing the same thing, it must be the right thing. We are not audacious enough to question because it's always been done this way.

This is how most of us end up being a victim of **THE BOX-LIFE SYNDROME.**

Think about it for a moment: most of us sleep through the night to wake up on a Box Bed. As soon as we wake up, we satiate our urge by peeping into our Box Mobile. We then take a shower in a Box Cubicle.

We eat breakfast out of a Box because we are in a hurry to reach the office, in a car which, yes, is another Box.

The office is nothing but a big Box broken down into smaller boxes (cubicles) where we end up sitting and staring at an even smaller box called a computer.

It doesn't end here.

We have our lunch in a box, type, and talk to others through a box (Mobile).

After the stipulated time at the office Box is over, we again get into the box with four wheels and reach the house Box. We then spend the rest of our time in front of the Box television.

Then again, we sleep on the Box bed.

It seems to be an infinite loop.

At this point you may realise, you're living in too many 'BOX'es, isn't it? And this is how most of us are living without even thinking.

The question is whether this is the correct way of living?

The answer should be obvious once we analyse the outcome.

If this is the right framework of living, then most of us should be living a life full of passion, joy, fulfilment, and meaning – an Epic Life.

But both you and I know that's certainly not true.

It is so easy to see that.

It is incredibly frustrating when we realise that we followed all the rules that society laid down for us. We did everything that was expected of us.

We went to school and got ourselves the standard education. We started working like everybody else. We got married. We started a family. We made kids. We followed the formula to the T.

So, where is the lacuna?

Why don't we feel fulfilled and have a life of meaning?

We are working so hard, but most of us are not even close to living the life of our dreams.

Look around, and you'll see: Most people are not as happy as they want to be. Most people are not fit and healthy. Most people are not in the relationship they want. Most people are not earning what they want to earn. In a nutshell, most people are not living the life they want.

To be honest, most people haven't even taken the time to figure out what they REALLY want. We've somehow messed up our life wherein we have infinite demands on our time and energy. We are living a life of urgency and stress, where we are overwhelmed and almost exhausted.

The Box-life is like running on a treadmill expecting to get somewhere. But no matter how much or how fast we run, there is no destination whatsoever. We are too busy running even to realise how disappointed we are with our current way of living.

Simply put, the Box-life framework is not working!

The Box-life framework of society isn't designed to produce passion, joy, fulfilment, and meaning. It's designed to produce a life of mediocrity, which leads to massive disappointment because it lacks purpose and meaning.

In essence, to be truly living a life of joy, fulfilment with purpose and meaning - is an exception and not the standard.

If we want to be the exception and not the standard, we need to take back control of our lives. We need to stop following mindlessly because it is evident that most people don't know how to create an Epic Life.

> 66 *"Most folks tiptoe through life only to make it safely to death."*
>
> — *Eleanor Roosevelt.*

To have a truly Epic life, you need to think outside the BOX. You need to take time out, and you need to ask yourself:

- What is the purpose of my life?
- What is the meaning of my life?
- Why am I doing what I am doing?
- What do I genuinely seek out of life?
- Why do I even exist?

Come on, don't just read through. Take some time out to ask yourself these questions before you proceed.

Most of us have no idea why we exist. It is not due to the absence of an answer, but because we haven't taken the time to figure it out (from our so-called busy lives).

Let's figure it out and do the heavy-lifting now.

THE PURPOSE OF LIFE

First of all, I must congratulate you!

Most people who are living the Box Life never bother about the purpose of life. Just thinking about and questioning the purpose of your life brings you a step closer to breaking free from the shackles of mediocrity.

Secondly, I regret to inform you that I do not know and have not come across a fixed formula or framework that can be memorised and routinely applied to determine your purpose in life.

Think about this, at the end of life; it doesn't really matter how much money or status we have. Most people are forgotten, and we all end up dying as a pile of dust. What then, is the Purpose of life?

But before we jump to a conclusion, let us also find out what the great thinkers and philosophers have to say about the Purpose of life.

Interestingly, if we could somehow get all the great thinkers from all the generations together and asked them what the purpose of life is, they would probably come to the same conclusion: **the purpose of life is to be HAPPY.**

> *Happiness is the meaning and the purpose of life, the whole aim and end of human existence."*
> **—Aristotle (Born in 322 B.C.)**

> *I believe that the very purpose of life is to be happy."*
> **—Dalai Lama (Born in 1935 A.D.)**

Aristotle and the Dalai Lama belonged to different cultures, different religions, different philosophies, and they had a time gap of more than 2300 years.

The world's dynamic has changed in the past 2300 years, but they both had the same opinion: The very purpose of life is to be happy.

Think about this for a moment.

What would you say if I asked you what your ultimate dream in life is?

You might say that my dream is to make a million or a billion dollars.

You might say that my dream is to raise my children to be good human beings who are happy and healthy individuals. To raise children who can make a difference in their own lives and the lives of those they touch.

You might say, my dream is to travel all around the world and stay at the best accommodations that money can buy.

You may not want any of the above and say that your dream is to make a massive difference in the lives of people you know.

Now I'm going to stop you right there and ask you, why do you think you want any of it?

Why would you work so hard to support your children and want them to be good people?

Why do you want to travel around the world and stay at the best accommodations?

Why is it that you want to earn that kind of money and get the Lamborghini or the Ferrari?

What's really behind it all?

The answer is simple.

We desire and crave meaningful relationships, money and wealth, fame and power, beauty, and good health because we assume that we shall feel happier once we have it.

Now you're going to say: "Really Koonal, you think you're a genius to figure that out and that I didn't already know that? Thanks for wasting my time."

I get that.

I know that intellectually you know that happiness is the real purpose of life.

You would even mock me if I said that happiness is within you right now, and you don't have to do anything to experience true happiness.

You would say, "Come on Koonal, I know that. Isn't it common sense!?"

We all know it's better to stop worrying about making a million dollars or how to impress friends and influence people. We all know it's more beneficial to find ways to make everyday life more harmonious and satisfying.

But then I might ask you, why don't you be happy?

To which you might answer, "Well, I am happy."

But are you really happy all the time?

I know I am not!

But I am getting way better than I was before because now I know how the brain functions and when we feel happiest.

What if you too could find out what makes you the happiest so that you could easily multiply it and experience it more consistently?

Wouldn't that be a life well lived?

No doubt about it!

So, let's just jump into deconstructing happiness.

Sonja Lyubormirsky, a renowned professor in the Department of Psychology at the University of California, suggested strategies backed by scientific research that can be used to increase happiness.

If an unhappy person wants to experience interest, enthusiasm, passion, fulfilment, peace, and joy, he or she can make it happen by learning the habits of a happy person.

And if we observe patterns in happy people, we shall find that they do not just sit around hoping to find happiness within. They make things happen. They pursue new understandings, seek new achievements, and control their thoughts and feelings.

She concludes that, "In a nutshell, the fountain of happiness can be found in how you behave, what you think, and what goals you set every day of your life."

Even Abraham Maslow, best known for creating the hierarchy of need, echoes the same feeling. He says inner peace and meaning, fulfilment and happiness can only come from "self-actualisation." He beautifully said, **"What one can be, one must be!"**

Simply stated, according to Abraham Maslow, happiness, meaning, and fulfilment comes from a place where one is challenging himself and pursuing his full potential.

If you doubt this, think about one of the happiest moments in your life.

More often than not, it would be a moment when you achieved something fulfilling and meaningful by stretching and challenging yourself. It would have been a moment when you not only met or satisfied a need but also stretched beyond and achieved something unexpected of you.

Now, in Potential Story, we discovered that we have the infinite potential within us. How can we relate this to our purpose in life?

They are two sides of the same coin as it is our constant quest to grow and try to live true to our potential. To keep exploring what we are capable of doing. That's how you derive true happiness.

Take a moment to ponder, why do we keep wanting more happiness, more success, more passion, more productivity, more energy, more meaning? It is because the potential within us wants to grow and express itself.

If you run, you want to run faster.

If you jump, you want to jump higher.

If you play a sport, you want to play better!

To sum it all up, the TRUE PURPOSE of life is happiness through expansion and fuller expression of our infinite potential.

As Maslow appropriately puts it, "What one can be, one must be!"

It all adds up now and makes sense – Who we are and why we exist.

Now, this might all sound good and philosophical, but we all know of people who derive happiness by having alcohol or cocaine and care two hoots about growth and potential.

We all know of people who are lazy and derive happiness by sleeping all day long and gossiping.

Yes, they do get happiness, but the question is, for how long?

These are strategies and ways of living that people indulge in to derive pleasure. They try and change the way they feel in the moment, i.e., to make themselves feel good and feel happy.

But the problem is none of them works long term, even the pleasure derived from the highest high that a person can get from cocaine only lasts for a short period of time.

Pleasure is an essential component of quality of life, but it does not bring any happiness. At best, pleasure helps you release the stress of the Box-life syndrome but only temporarily.

True and lasting happiness is derived when a person's body or mind is stretched to its limits to accomplish something difficult and worthwhile. Something that challenges him to unleash his potential. This pursuit of accomplishment is what people call ENJOYMENT.

In all stories and fables, before the Hero could ENJOY living happily ever after, he had to unleash his potential and challenge the fiery dragons. This metaphor applies to life as well.

I request you to stop right here and ask yourself if achievement is everything, then is all the talk about inner happiness a sham?

Not really.

This brings us to the Ultimate Happiness Formula.

The Ultimate Happiness Formula

The Ultimate Happiness Formula is (what I call) being in a state of F.I.S.H.

What does F.I.S.H stand for?

F| Feeling

I | Incredibly

S| Satisfied and

H| Hungry for more.

Each of us is hungry to achieve or accomplish something. How close we get to attain that vision becomes the measure of the quality of our lives.

If it remains beyond reach, we grow resentful or disappointed; if it is at least in part achieved, we experience a sense of happiness, joy, fulfilment and meaning.

However, suppose one is only hungry for more (wealth, power, and fame) and somehow ends up becoming a powerful and influential millionaire. Still, even then, he will find himself back to square one, with a new list of wishes and end up being just as dissatisfied as he was before.

Hence, in the formula and also in life, satisfaction must come before hunger. Otherwise, one may end up having a low quality of life wherein one is always focusing on things he doesn't have instead of appreciating and being in gratitude for what he does.

What does satisfaction even mean?

Satisfaction is the art of communicating with oneself, where one feels grateful for what he already has. He communicates to himself that he has enough right now and is truly blessed.

He says to himself, "I don't want, I have; I don't need, I have, and I am incredibly thankful for that."

Then again, only satisfaction doesn't make the cut too.

If one is only satisfied, there is no zeal, no passion, and nothing to work for and look forward to in life.

One has to consciously be hungry and intend to expand his life even more from here. One has to strive more to serve others, and as a result, gain more wealth and abundance for himself and his family every single day.

Therefore, the formula also acknowledges the relevance of being hungry for achievement, such as money, fame, wealth and power to long term happiness. Achievements are a genuine blessing, but only if these achievements help us feel better and happy. Otherwise, they are only a hurdle to a good quality of life.

PENDULUM OF HAPPINESS

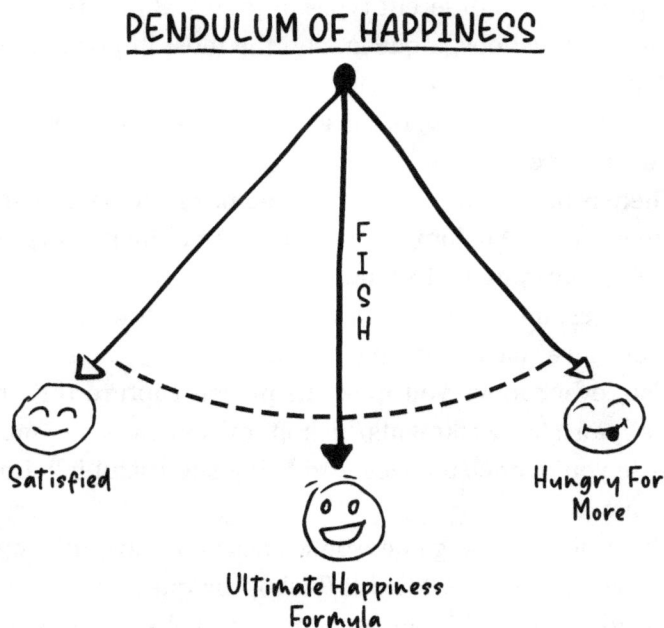

F
I
S
H

Satisfied

Hungry For
More

Ultimate Happiness
Formula

The formula keeps happiness as the primary focus. It entails striving for growth by being hungry but also enjoying the process by being satisfied with what we already have.

This is the magic formula for happiness!

MEANING OF LIFE

Now that we know what the purpose of life is, which dictionary do we search to comprehend the 'Meaning of Life'?

Surprisingly, there are none that help us get there.

There is no meaning to life unless YOU give meaning to your life.

Let me take an example of a game called chess to drive the point home.

Have you ever played chess?

If you haven't, let me tell you that in a game of chess, each player has 6 different types of pieces: 8 pawns, 2 rooks, 2 knights, 2 bishops, a queen, and the most important one – the king.

The primary purpose of the game of chess is to capture and kill the opponent's king.

There is no meaning in playing a game of chess if the moves you make are not helping you towards the ultimate purpose of capturing the opponent's king.

However, once you have a vision of this ultimate purpose, all your moves have meaning and start making sense.

Also, every move you make helps you capture the opponent's pawn/rooks/knights/bishop or queen is a success because you're one step closer to being successful in winning the game.

While playing the game, sometimes you may have to sacrifice the pawn/rooks/knights/bishop or queen because you have eyes on your ultimate outcome, and believe that winning is worth the sacrifice.

To begin with, life is no different than a game of chess. There is no meaning to life if you keep living the BOX-LIFE aimlessly. But, once you have a vision of what you ultimately want - all your actions and all your days start having meaning.

This meaning aligns with your purpose because the vision is nothing but an expansion and fuller expression of your potential.

Every small achievement towards the vision is a success in itself. It helps us get one step closer to being successful in winning the game of life.

It turns out, like in the game of chess, the purpose and the end result of having a vision of what you ultimately want and working towards it, is worth dying for.

No wonder Martin Luther King said, if you have not discovered something worth dying for, your life isn't worth living for.

Having said that, there is one massive difference between the game of chess and life!

The game of chess comes with specified objectives and instructions.

On the other hand, unlike chess, we were not born with an instruction manual. Consequently, we have no knowledge of what a successful and epic life should look like.

So how do you know when you are successful in the game of life?

Your vision of an Epic life is YOUR VISION of an EPIC LIFE. You are FREE to DISCOVER what it should look like.

All you need to do is take some time out and dig deep within yourself to access the real thoughts that control your desires and motivations and ask yourself what you really want?

You need to Turn-off the notifications of your cell phones, emails, social media and Turn-On the notifications of your desires, hopes, and motivations.

In short, you need to make your heart your new brain.

No wonder the wise amongst us have always said - Follow Your Heart.

Does the idea of designing your life sound exciting?

If yes, let us now start the process of visioneering and designing our Epic life plan.

EPIC LIFE FORMULA (E.L.F)

So, what is an Epic Life?

I define an Epic life as an extraordinary life where one can derive happiness from having it all. It is a manifestation of all our dreams, ambitions, and motivations.

It's where we squeeze out all the juice that life has to offer, and we succeed in all areas of life that truly matter.

Now you may wonder, what if we do not succeed in all the areas of our life? Can it not be Epic, then?

Sadly, no.

An Epic life is not having success in only one or two areas that matter.

For instance, having a lot of money but not having the health to enjoy wealth. Or having a lot of money and good health but not having the right people around to share the magical moments with.

A success in only one/few and not all areas of life will be a hollow victory, and a hollow victory is neither a happy nor an Epic Life.

Now, to get success and manifest our dreams, ambitions, and motivations in all areas that matter, we need to ask ourselves, what are the critical areas that truly matter?

Clarity on what we want is divine power, as it helps us develop a laser-sharp focus on what we want in life.

Once we can get clarity on what truly matters, then and only then can we focus on the same without being attracted to every shiny object that distracts our attention. Then and only then can we design our life and not live life by default.

I have deconstructed the foundational areas that I believe are most important to an Epic quality of life that we desire. I find them incredibly valuable, and I call them **'The Big 5'**. They are as follows:

- Health & Fitness
- Service to others/Career
- Love & Relationships
- Wealth & Experiences
- Interior Architecture

The Big 5

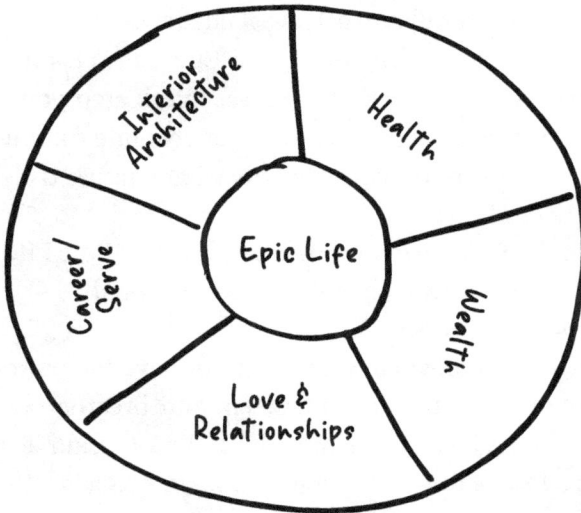

They encompass all the necessary aspects that can bring happiness to improve the quality of one's life.

Though you are free to choose or identify any other area that may seem important to you.

Remember, it's your life and not mine.

Once you have finalised the areas that are important to you, you can then decide to have an Epic Life Vision.

As achievers, we do not need any random vision. Instead, what we really need is to design an Epic Life Vision.

> 66 *The most pathetic person in the world is someone who has sight but has no vision."*
>
> **—Helen Keller**

Now, let's understand what an Epic life Vision is?

An Epic Life Vision is a vision that fuels your purpose and provides meaning to your life. It's a vision that is so compelling that you are driven to achieve it, no matter what. It's a vision that you are willing to die for. You will do whatever it takes and go through all the inevitable hurdles to achieve it anyhow.

If you can successfully design an Epic Life Vision, you can have your own yardstick of success. Every step you take towards your vision emanates a sense of absolute fulfilment and joy, as now you are moving towards what success truly means to YOU.

A word of caution: While designing the Epic Life Vision, please make sure it's truly epic and aspirational!

Why is that necessary?

Believe it or not, small visions do not have the power to stir our emotions, to make us eat, sleep, and breathe our vision. Sooner or later, a small vision will run out of steam, leaving us dry with a loss of impetus, passion, and enthusiasm.

That's also one of the problems with most people. They dream small, and because of that, they do not have the ants in their pants to get them going.

Ask yourself, what would motivate you to sleep late and get up early every day - Ten Thousand Dollars a month or 1 Million Dollars a month? (Kindly Note: I do not want you to be motivated by more money in your bank. But think of money as a resource for what you could do with it for your family and people you genuinely care about).

Long story short, our epic life vision should be something that motivates us and inspires us to take massive and relentless action.

One more thing!

A big and compelling vision won't stand pace without an even more powerful and compelling reason for you to achieve it!

Let's admit it; the journey to achieve our Epic Life Vision wouldn't be an easy one. If it were easy, everyone would be living one.

If you are eyeing something big and monumental, chances are, more often than not, you will have to encounter a lot of obstacles, failures, and rejections on your way.

In such a scenario, if you do not have a compelling reason for you to achieve the Epic Vision, you will let go of it when things are not going as per plan. Without a compelling reason, you might end up saying, 'let it be, life is good as it is.'

Hence, to stick to it, you must tape all leaks by asking yourself, **"Why is it absolutely necessary for me to achieve my Epic Life vision?"**

Ultimate Advantage Pro-tip

You must attach enough pain and negative consequences to NOT achieving your Epic Life vision. The unbearable pain of not having the Epic Life will drive you to keep going, no matter what.

What do I mean by attaching pain to not achieving your vision?

Let me give you an example of how I attach pain to my vision.

I feel I will be doing injustice to my daughter, my wife, my parents, and loved ones if I cannot give them a life of abundance. The very thought of not being able to provide them with a life of abundance shakes me up. That's what keeps me going even when I want to give up.

Does it make sense?

I hope it does!

In short, an Epic Life Vision should be:

1. Aspirational and
2. Have a compelling reason for you to achieve it.

Now, let's get cracking.

THE BIG 5: YOUR OWN SUCCESS SCORECARD

Health and Fitness

Health and fitness is by far one of the MOST important and simple areas and is also by far the most ignored one.

Research shows that proper health, powered by exercise, nutrition, and sleep, significantly increases our ability to think clearly. So if we care about the way we think and analyse, we must focus on our health and fitness.

Also, science has proved time and again that if the body is rested, properly fuelled, and hydrated, we are emotionally better off than when it is not. If you want to be in a happy state and not have unwanted emotions like stress, anxiety, and depression, you better focus on health and fitness.

Being in great shape and having great energy can have a profound impact on love life. It increases your admiration for each other and the quality of experiences you have with each other.

If you want to be a good parent, you must set a good example in front of your kids. Thus, teaching our kids about health and nutrition is one of our primary responsibility as a parent.

Having a high-powered career where you go all out to unleash and maximise your full potential is not only an intellectual challenge but also a physical one. It will require energy, strength, and stamina to propel your career forward.

All in all, to manifest our potential for (2) Service to others/ Career, (3) Love and Relationships, (4) Wealth, and (5) Interior Architecture, we have to focus and manifest our potential on our health and fitness.

Does it mean we MUST have a chiselled and athletic physique?

Absolutely no!

You may choose to have a vision where you have a chiselled body, but all we need for an Epic Life is a healthy body that is energised, rested, fuelled, and strong.

To give health and fitness the importance it deserves, we shall go more in-depth in chapter 5 – Physiology.

Think about it:
How would you envision your Health and fitness to be in your Epic Life Vision? Why is it absolutely important for you to achieve it?

Service to others/Career

To serve others is by far the most crucial area of the Epic Life. Every living being on this planet is serving others in some capacity or the other. This area deserves the most amount of time, attention, and consciousness to ensure all other facets can run smoothly.

Now, what are the ways in which one can serve?

We can broadly classify serving others into:

Serve to support

For instance, a stay at home parent or homemaker has to serve by being a caretaker, a cook, a chauffeur, a friend, a teacher without any financial benefit. For some roles, serving to support others may be the sole path to your epic life. It's fantastic and rewarding!

Ask yourself how you would like to serve others without expecting any financial benefit? How would you want to make the world a better place?

Serve to Generate Financial Benefit/Career

Money is like a sixth sense, without which you cannot make complete use of the other five."
– W Somerset Maugham.

In the culture and the modern era we live in, almost all of us need money to survive and enjoy life. If you don't have enough money, you will be missing out on a considerable amount of what life has to offer. We certainly need to make a good amount of money to have all the things and experiences we want.

Also, money is vital as it helps in eliminating suffering and poverty in this world. It keeps the human race moving forward.

It doesn't get more important, moving, and powerful than that.

Naturally then, money seems to be a subject that's on everybody's mind.

But have you ever wondered what 'Money' is?

Money is nothing but a symbol of our service. It's a symbol of all the good things we create and offer to the world. Money is generated by providing service and catering to the needs of other human beings.

Thus, to generate the maximum amount of money, we must serve others at the highest level we are capable of.

The greater our service, the greater our financial rewards.

Think about it:

In your Epic Life vision, how would you like to serve and generate the maximum wealth? Why is it absolutely necessary for you to achieve it?

Wealth/Quality of life

Wealth is one of the most rewarding facets. It's the icing on the cake. This is what we all think of when we imagine a life of abundance. It's about living life first class.

We are lucky to be living in an era with so many advancements to make life better, comfortable, and definitely more enjoyable. To live a life full of abundance and luxury is a privilege, and we all deserve it.

How do you want to enjoy the one life that you've been gifted? How do you want your epic life to look in terms of things you own and experiences you enjoy, by yourself and with your loved ones?

It's time to have your bucket list ready.

Remember, the money we earn through service is not an end in itself. It's a means to an end. What we truly want money for is to enjoy rewards in terms of:

1. The material things we want – wine collection, art collection, fancy cars, jewellery, watches, bags, etc.
2. The experiences we want – hobbies we wish to pursue, exotic travel, fine dining at Michelin star restaurants, wine or golf tours, theatres, plays, etc.
3. The environments we want to be surrounded by - Dream House or a Dream Workplace.

Surrounding oneself with beautiful things and create fantastic experiences can change and enhance your life in unique ways. They can help you have spiritual and emotional breakthroughs.

Experiences help you evolve and make you more interesting and knowledgeable as a person. Experiences last a lifetime, and they make life worth living. For instance, travel educates you like nothing else. It changes your viewpoint and the way you see the world.

Love and Relationships

Love and Relationships is one of the most fulfilling and rewarding areas. More than any other facet of the big 5, your relationships will determine your happiness and the quality of your life.

If you have fantastic relations with your spouse, parents, friends, children, and colleagues - that's where you will get the most enjoyment out of life.

Time spent with loved ones provides you with the best memories and all the wonderful feelings that you're after.

Having poor relationships makes you suffer the most. It gives you stress, pain, anger, guilt, frustrations, and all the feelings that will pull you down.

Fundamentally, relationships are about people interacting with each other. It's about (hopefully) enjoying each other's company on life's journey trying to meet each other's needs at a certain level.

Every good and healthy relationship should yield something positive for both people involved.

Think about it:
What kind of relationships do you envision in your Epic Life Vision? Why is it absolutely necessary for you?

Interior Architecture

> ❝ *Those who travel outward seek completeness in things;*
> *those who gaze inward find sufficiency in themselves."*
> — *Liezi, The Book of Master Lie*

What if you have everything you desire in the world, and you're still not happy?

Would that be an Epic Life?

Certainly not!

Interior Architecture is often the most ignored facet but is a facet that profoundly impacts our lives. Almost nobody looks at what they are on the inside.

But beware, without proper Interior Architecture, one cannot truly enjoy the benefits of an Epic Life.

An Epic Life can only be enjoyed inside out and not the other way around. What's going on within us is so fundamentally important to enjoy life.

The Interior Architecture that we must master for an Epic quality of Life are:

- Your mindset and the way you think
- Your Emotions that controls the way you feel
- Your Inner Nature and Character

Your mindset and the way you think

> To enjoy good health, to bring true happiness to one's family, to bring peace to all, one must first discipline and control one's own mind. If a man can control his mind, he can find the way to Enlightenment, and all wisdom and virtue will naturally come to him."
>
> — *Buddha*

You'll never rise higher in the world than the way you see yourself!

How would you like to see yourself and the world around you?

Would you want to focus on the good side of life or the bad side of life?

Would you rather be a volcano of positivity or an abyss of negativity?

Just imagine, even if 1000 things are going well and positive in your life, and only one negative, where does all your focus tend to go?

More often than not, the one negative aspect overpowers 1000 positive things. That's how the brain is designed to function.

Remember, Stress and Challenge are sewn into the fabric of life.

Life will give us 1000 reasons to sit on the couch and cry all day. Would you cry, or would you want to get up and rock the boat?

A positive mindset to count your blessings over cursing your fate is a fundamental piece in the puzzle of making a world-class Interior Architecture. That's a mindset we should look forward to in an epic life!

When you envision your Epic Life, how would you like to think? Why is it absolutely necessary for you to think that way?

How would you like to feel?

It's shocking to know that even the biggest of accomplishments on the outside will never be able to fill even the smallest void inside.

What does that even mean?

What it means is this: If we continue to muster feelings of pain, guilt, anger, hatred, jealousy, and resentment inside, if we are full of toxicity and are stuck with what has happened in the past, nothing will ever feel right.

We may be having a positive mindset, but the negative feelings repressed and suppressed within us will sabotage our enjoyment. The lacuna within us can only be bridged by releasing the old emotions we have bottled up, and which do not serve us anymore.

To truly enjoy the life you create, can you let go of all the negative feelings?

Can you forgive people who may have hurt you in the past?

To truly savour the life you create, can you let go of envy and celebrate the success of others around you?

Remember, you are running your own race of success; their success shouldn't affect you.

We have to fill our holes to feel WHOLE!

Think about it:

When you envision your Epic Life, how would you like to continuously and consistently feel? Why is it absolutely necessary for you to feel this way?

What kind of a person do you want to become?

Last but most important, how would you envision your future best self to be like?

What kind of character traits and inner nature would you want?

That's an intriguing question but first, let us understand what character is.

Our character trait/inner nature is our identity; it is the foundation of who we are. Who we are on the inside determines how we live on the outside.

The character is a mark on your soul. It is everything that you are!

To better answer the above question, you may like to think of how you would like your friends and loved ones to describe your ideal self.

You may want them to describe you as honest, friendly, helpful, reliable, courageous, compassionate, knowledgeable, enthusiastic, trustworthy, etc.

> *Every man is free to rise as far as he is willing or able. But the degree to which he thinks will determine the degree to which he'll rise."*
>
> *— Ayn Rand*

Does The Big 5 make sense to you? All facets of The Big 5 are deeply connected. They support each other and are supported by each other. We need excellence in all five categories to enjoy an epic quality of life.

Epic Life Formula (ELF) entails striving to reach your full potential and excellence in every vital area of your life. It helps you get rid of the regret of not doing things you should have done!

> *Regret for the things we did can be tempered by time. It is regret for the things we didn't do that are inconsolable."*
>
> *— Sydney J. Harris.*

FLIGHT OF FANTASY: LIFE DESIGN SYSTEM

> " *All men dream: but not equally. Those who dream by night in the dusty recesses of their minds wake up in the day to find it was vanity, but the dreamers of the day are dangerous men, for they may act their dreams with open eyes, to make it possible.*"
> — **T.E.Lawrence (Lawrence of Arabia.)**

Now, most of us are struggling even to pay our monthly bills, and thus the very idea of having an EPIC LIFE seems like a daydream.

Exactly my point.

Remember, Epic life Vision is about creating your ideal life, first on paper, and then progressing towards it every day. This is what gives meaning to life.

All we want to do is to get connected to what we want and what we love. Just being aware of that is a powerful ideal.

Maybe, being aware of the Epic life gets us all excited and passionate. Perhaps someday we begin designing our Epic Life v/s living a life of default.

We do not have to quit everything and do it full time.

Rather, we do not have to devote any energy, resource, or time to the idea's execution. All that we want now is to have a vision of what we would desire our life to be like.

Maybe, once we know what we truly want, we start looking for ways to do it. Maybe paths, projections, and directions start becoming apparent.

Maybe we start experimenting on weekends or during evenings (after work). Perhaps we might eventually find a way to do it full time.

Maybe when we connect with the best that's available inside of us, and we nurture our gifts and talents, one day we may wake up and find ourselves Living the Epic Life.

We do not know what we will do with it yet. The idea is to have a vision of what an Epic Life would look like.

This is the point where I want to take you on an exciting journey, on a Flight of Fantasy.

Let's get started!

Imagine that you are at an airport and you are about to board your flight.

It's a special flight where you're not allowed to take with you any stress, concern, exhaustion, or workload. Before you take the flight, you have to let go of every concern that you may have in any area of your life.

You have passed the security check, and you are clean; you feel incredibly light. You let go of all the emotional baggage from the past, and the anxiety of the future.

You have boarded the flight and are bursting with excitement and enthusiasm.

Imagine the flight taking off and reaching the highest altitude. Imagine the flight moving towards a beaming source of light. Imagine reaching the source of ultimate energy.

It's such a beautiful place. Everything here is soothing, from the sounds you hear to the sights you see, to the fragrance you smell. If there was heaven, this was it.

You have reached the source of ultimate energy. You have access to all the resources you'll ever need, and you can choose to have anything, ANYTHING you want.

It's the rare air of opportunity where whatever you desire will come true. Every wish is floating freely, and you can choose whatever you want.

What do you really want?

Remember, you can choose whatever you want. This is the source of ultimate energy. You do not have to think about whether it's possible or not!

This is your personal flight of fantasy.

What would you want your health to look like?

What would you want your love and relationships to be like?

What would you want your career to be like?

What would you want your wealth to be like?

What would you want your persona to be like?

How would you like to contribute and give back to the world?

Take some time out from your busy schedule and take the flight of fantasy to create the vision of your Epic Life.

When you take the flight of fantasy, do not think how you would achieve it. And write every detail and be as specific as you can be.

While you choose what you want, do not, I repeat, DO NOT think of how you're going to get it. Do not think about the money, energy, resource, or time you need to achieve it. Just have a vision of what you want.

Please note, you might not be able to decide what you want in the first go. Do not hurry while discovering what you want.

Remember, it's your EPIC LIFE that we are talking about.

Check-list of your Epic Life Vision

Is the Epic Life vision a vision that I've NEVER done or achieved before?	Yes/No
Am I clueless as to how I will achieve my Epic Life Vision?	Yes/No
To achieve the Epic Life vision, will I have to challenge myself, and will I have to go all out?	Yes/No
Is it something that I desperately want?	Yes/No

Do I have a strong and compelling reason to want it?	Yes/No
Is the vision compelling enough for me to wake up every morning and get excited? Is the vision worth dying for?	Yes/No

If the answer to any of the above questions is a NO, it is not an Epic Life Vision. You will have to keep repeating the exercise until all the answers to the above questions is an emphatic YES!

Once you have the vision, you have to make a committed decision to keep working towards it.

We now know what success is to us. We can now give meaning to life by spending every waking hour of our life in pursuit of our Epic vision.

The Epic vision is fantastic.

But you're probably wondering, 'HOW' are you going to accomplish it?

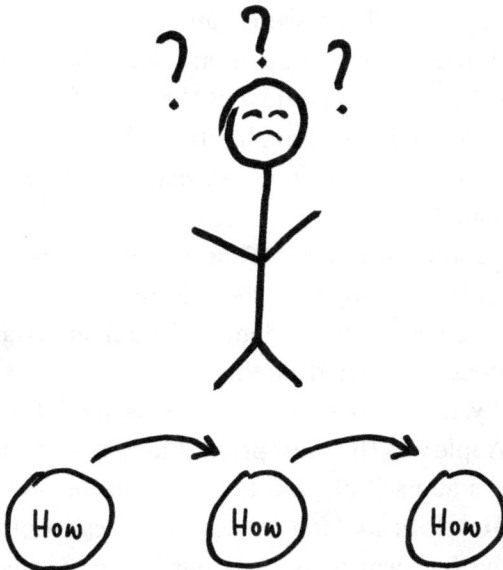

S.W.A.T. THE 'HOW'!

> *Nothing is created, and nothing is destroyed,*
> *but everything is transformed."*
> — *Antoine-Laurent de Lavoisier*

It is natural for you to think that the Epic Life is beyond your reach.

HOW, I mean, HOW will you achieve it?

We shall answer the How in the chapters to come, but before we proceed, I would request you to STOP WONDERING AND THINKING (S.W.A.T) about the How.

Interestingly, no one who has ever achieved anything significant ever knew the 'how' before achieving it. The 'how' has always been a mystery, but that never stopped them from achieving it.

Think about it. Did the Wright Brothers know HOW they would invent the aircraft?

No, they did not. They only imagined flying.

The Wright Brothers were labelled as mad and were ridiculed by everyone around them. They had no resources available at their disposal to invent the aircraft.

If they wondered and thought about the HOW, they would have never been able to change the course of history and give us access to another world.

Did Steve Jobs know HOW he would create the world's most profitable company sitting in his garage?

No, he imagined making a dent in the universe (not literally) and was obsessed with getting there!

Eventually, after a lot of ups and downs, he did get there. He made sure Apple was the most profitable company in the world.

Steve Jobs sums it all beautifully when he says; you can't **connect the dots** looking forward; you can only **connect** them looking backwards. So you have to trust that the dots will somehow connect in your future. You have to trust in something – your gut, destiny, life, karma, whatever.

> *The man who misses all the fun*
> *Is he who says, "It can't be done."*
> *In solemn pride he stands aloof*
> *And greets each venture with reproof.*
>
> *Had he the power, he'd efface*
> *The history of the human race.*
> *We'd have no radio or motor cars*
> *No streets lit by electric stars.*
>
> *No telegraph nor telephone*
> *We'd linger in the age of stone.*
> *The world would sleep if things were run*
> *By men who say, "It can't be done."*

—William J. Bennett

Ask yourself if they can do it, why not you?

If the super achievers could get whatever they imagined, I see no reason why you, given your infinite potential, cannot live your vision of the Epic life you desire.

If you can imagine it, you too can have it.

I urge you to look around once. Everything you see around you was once imagined by someone. Had they wondered and thought about the 'how,' they would have never been able to get what they wanted.

Without imagination, the world would have never evolved; it would have never progressed.

Think about the smartphone that you hold in your hand. Could it be invented when Jesus Christ was alive?

Of Course, yes.

All the resources required to make the smartphone were always available.

It's just that no one imagined it and discovered the process of how to do it. The real game is about being aware of what one wants.

Once someone imagined it, the Smart Phone we hold in our hands today got created.

Remember, the how of achievement only comes through trial and error.

So, as of now, let's Stop Wondering and Thinking (S.W.A.T.) 'HOW'.

The only thing you should be worried and thinking about is whether you are willing to pay the price and do whatever it takes to achieve your Epic Life Vision.

Unfortunately, there are no free lunches in the world.

Remember, given the potential available within you, the question is not, "CAN YOU DO IT?"

The vital question is, "WILL YOU do whatever it takes to unleash your ultimate advantage?".

If the answer to the above is yes, then and only then proceed to read the chapters ahead, where we get tactical with the strategies required to make your vision a reality.

To make our Dream our Reality, we must A.C.T on our Dream of the Epic Life Vision because only Actions Create Transformations (A.C.T.)

Dreams do inspire, but inspiration without implementation is a mere illusion! We must relentlessly A.C.T if we want to make a journey from 'the way we live' to 'the way we want to live.' PERIOD!

Start your ACT by jumping to the next chapter, which shall help you develop the optimum...

THREE

PSYCHE

Reprogramming The Mind To Manifest The Result You Desire

> *What you think you become. What you feel you attract. What you imagine you create."*
> **—Buddha**

How many times have you had an 'AHA!' moment (i.e. a moment of sudden insight or discovery) wherein you told yourself, "Enough is enough! From this day onwards:

I am going to diet so that I will lose weight, or
I am going to work hard so that I can earn more money, or
I am going to give more time so that I can enjoy a fulfilling relationship, or
I am going to stop worrying and start living!"

I am almost certain that like me, you too have had multiple 'AHA!' moments.

When we commit to change, we are all pumped up and very optimistic about making a lasting change in our lives.

But why is it that we cannot sustain the decisions that can transform our life?

Why is it that when we reflect upon our lives a week or month later, we see we are back to square one?

These 'AHA!' moments are thrilling but are cheap! They do have the power to transform our lives, but more often than not, they usually fade and fizzle out.

And you know what? Inspite of not having the desired result and not sticking to our commitment, we are not very disappointed. Would you want to know why?

It is because though we were hoping for a better version of ourselves, but deep down, within our core, we somewhat knew that it wasn't going to happen anyway.

Did you have an 'AHA!' moment after designing your Epic Life Vision? Did it get you all excited and pumped up?

I bet you did.

However, you shall be able to journey from 'living the life you are living' to 'living the Epic Life', if and only if, you can make the vision a part of your daily lifestyle.

Instead of hoping that it happens somehow, or thinking that you are okay whether it happens or not; you have to burn your bridges and make it an absolute must.

What does it mean to 'burn your bridges'?

The above expression is derived from the idea of burning down a bridge after crossing it, leaving no choice but to continue on the march ahead.

Figuratively, it means a point of no return!

When you burn your bridges and decide something as an absolute must, you decide that you are either (1) going to find a way to make it happen or (2) create the way yourself. That's how you develop the optimum psychology required for success.

This simple concept of never settling for anything less and going for what you truly deserve, can change your mindset and help you achieve exponential success.

Tony Robbins (America's top life and business strategist) says, 'you are not getting what you want in life because you haven't made it an absolute must.'

Think about it: you never say, "I *should* go to work today" because you know that you *must* go to work or you'll lose your job. Hence, when things become a must, you find a way to do them even when it's painful or difficult.

When you burn your bridges and view your Epic Life Vision as an absolute must, you are committing to taking control over your life quality. You then progress from living the life you always have, towards living the life you want.

Now the big question is, how do you turn your vision into an absolute must?

To make the kind of commitment towards our Epic Life Vision that is consistent, meaningful, and lasts long-term; we have to first understand what drives lasting change at a deeper level.

Would you want to live your EPIC LIFE VISION by becoming an effective 'agent of change'?

If the answer is *yes*, then let's explore.

THE IDENTITY ICEBERG

Do you remember the ship named 'Titanic'?

What sank the titanic?

Yes, you're right; it was an iceberg.

The Titanic sunk because it hit a small mountain of ice that was bobbing above water.

But, do you think that small mountain of ice was the real reason why the Titanic went down?

Of course not!

It might have seemed that way to the naked eye, but that's only 3-5% of the story.

What sank the Titanic was the 95-97% of the iceberg that wasn't visible to the naked eye.

Now you would wonder, how does the sinking of the Titanic have any relevance here?

Let me explain.

When we have an 'AHA!' moment, we decide that we should alter our life and change something about the way we live, to achieve results we desire.

So, what do we change?

Like everything else, we try to change things that are visible to the naked eye i.e., we try to alter our actions, decisions and behaviour.

For instance, if someone decides "Enough is enough, I am going to diet so that I can lose 5 kgs in 3 months."

What does he do?

Based on the desired result, he decides to control and re-duce his calorie intake. He decides to change his behaviour from eating junk to protein-rich food that is low on calories. He decides to take action by not visiting McDonald's and (not) having the Happy Meal.

He decides to go for what I call D4+, i.e., being disciplined, determined, dedicated and desperate to lose weight.

What happens next?

Sooner or later, he realises that he is not able to control the urge. He maybe goes to a friend's birthday party, sees a tempting slice of cake and ends up eating it.

As soon as he has that slice of cake, he transitions from D4+ to **D4-, i.e. being dejected, depressed, disheartened and discouraged**. He feels he will always be fat.

Simply put, he ends up not getting the desired result.

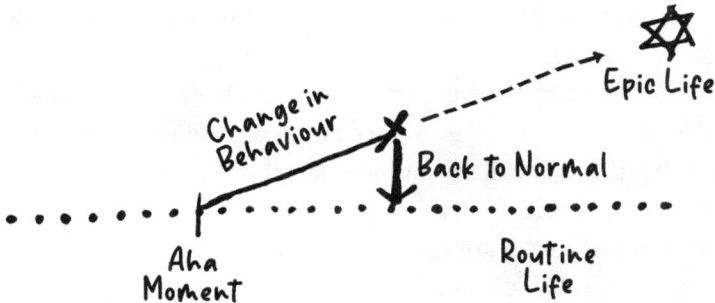

This almost always happens because what he was trying to change is only the observable parts of success: only the top 3-5%.

Unfortunately, the secret ingredient that leads to a real shift in results and long-term change (leading to growth and success) is the 95-97% of the iceberg that is not visible to the naked eye. Please make no mistake about it.

This secret ingredient is our 'subconscious mind'!

The 'subconscious mind' makes up our self-image, i.e. our identity - who we really are. (Does it ring a bell? Think: Potential Story)

The subconscious mind has immense power in controlling your life experiences - from the types of food you eat to the actions you take each day. It also affects how you react to stressful situations.

In short, you may think of the subconscious as the auto-pilot feature on an airplane. It has been pre-programmed to follow a specific route, and even if you deviate from that route, it will get you right back on the specified track.

Let us take the same example of a person trying to lose weight. While he is trying to lose weight, he may say to himself, "I'm going to lose weight this time, but you know what, I've always been obese!"

What do you think is the identity of that person in his subconscious?

It is evident that in his subconscious mind, his identity is of an obese person.

If his identity is of a person who is obese, then it doesn't matter how hard he tries, it's going to be pointless. Pretty soon, the subconscious will do course-correction (auto-pilot), and he will be back to his old habits.

It is because the subconscious is hard-wired to act in congruence with the self-image.

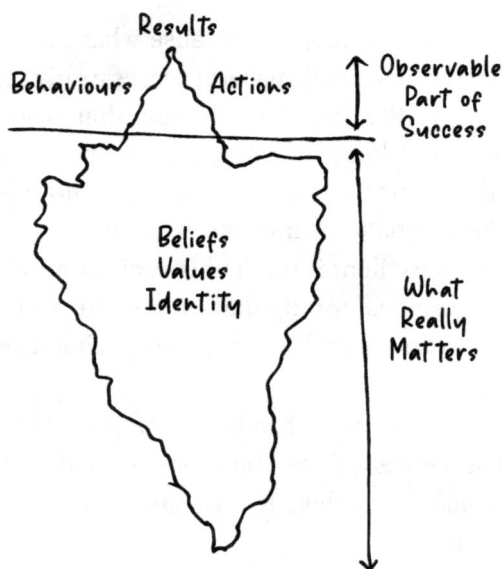

Look: if you want any real and everlasting change, you have to go deep and change your identity by altering your subconscious. It is the subconscious that has the power to make the Epic Life Vision an absolute must!

To sum it up, if the Epic Life Vision merely alters our decisions, behaviour, and actions, it will not result in any LASTING significant change in our life.

If we want the Epic Life vision to stick, we have to go deep and make it a part of our subconscious, i.e., the mind, spirit and soul – Our psyche. We have to shift our identity from the old to a new one that is in congruence with the Epic Life Vision.

So, how do we do it?

THE MARVELLOUS AND MIRACULOUS MIND

Let us play a small game.

May I request you to think of a black cat?

If you did think about the black cat, an image of a black cat might have appeared on the screen of your mind.

Now quickly think of your car. I am almost certain that an image of your vehicle may have appeared on the screen of your mind.

Now, think of someone you love. Did an image of the loved one appear?

Think of your favourite food or your favourite colour.

Can you see how fast you can switch from one image to another?

Last but not least, may I request you to think of your mind!

Most likely, when you think of your mind, an image of the brain may have cropped up on your mental screen.

A common mistake most people make is that they assume that the mind and the brain are the same things.

Surprisingly, the brain is not the mind. The brain is the most complex organ in the human body. Though the brain controls all the functions in the body, it is still an organ, just like the hands, legs or for that matter, the tongue.

Despite the mind being an eternal part of our being, no one has ever been able to see or verify the mind till date. Some say the mind is what's left when you subtract the brain and the rest of the body. The mind is a part of the soul.

The mind is the real identity, and the body is an extension of it. Everything happens in mind: pleasure, pain, happiness, sadness, contentment, discomfort, etc. In fact, the entire universe resides in our mind. But we don't know where the mind resides.

To have a better understanding, think of the cell phone that you use to make calls.

What do you think enables you to make a call?

You might say, a sim card.

Though, is it?

Can you make a call without a network provider?

Obviously not. Though you may not be able to see or feel the network, it has almost absolute control over whether you can make a call or not.

To get a clearer picture, you can think of the cell phone as the body, the sim card as the brain and the 'invisible network' which enables you to make the call – the mind!

Let us now understand how the mind and the body works. (Please note that though the mind works on multiple levels, for the simplicity of our understanding we shall deal with only two levels.)

- The Conscious mind (invisible)
- The Sub-conscious mind. (invisible)
- The Physical body (Visible)

CONSCIOUS VS SUB CONSCIOUS MIND

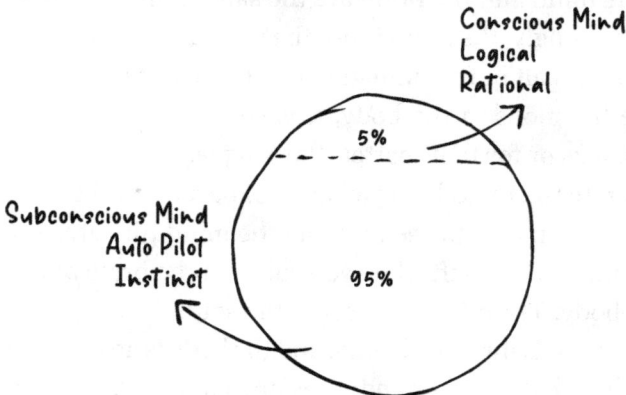

Conscious Mind
Logical
Rational

5%

Subconscious Mind
Auto Pilot
Instinct

95%

The Conscious Mind

The conscious mind is the rational and logical part of the mind. It is responsible for awareness and thinking with reason. It includes the things that we are thinking about right now. If we're aware of it, then it's in the conscious mind.

A little confused?

Think of it this way: right now, you're primarily using your conscious mind to read these words and absorb their meaning.

We use the conscious mind when we receive information from any of our 5 senses (Sight, Sound, Smell, Taste, and Touch). It helps to analyse the information, and then make decisions based on this information.

To top it off, the conscious mind has the ability to choose.

What does the ability to choose mean?

Think about it; you may choose to accept or reject the idea that I am proposing to you now. It's your free will, and that's the conscious mind at work.

The Sub-Conscious Mind

The 'subconscious' is the emotional mind that operates below your normal level of awareness.

In your conscious mind, you had the power to consciously choose (1) to accept and believe or (2) to reject and negate the idea.

Once you choose to accept or reject an idea consciously, it is then impressed upon the subconscious mind which now forms opinions, beliefs, values and habits. That's how the meaning-making machine (which we discussed in Potential Story) works.

But one thing's for sure, unlike the conscious mind, the subconscious mind is totally deductive.

What does being deductive mean?

Being deductive means that the subconscious mind cannot decide whether to choose or reject the idea. If the conscious mind accepts the idea, the subconscious mind has to accept it.

No wonder, the subconscious is often referred to as the 'God-Like' part of you. It knows no limits, except the ones which you consciously impose on yourself. This subconscious is genuinely magnificent.

The subconscious controls the physical body through all our actions and reactions.

For instance, how would you react if someone comes and slaps hard at you right now?

On the face of it, that reaction is going to be automatic without any conscious thought. That reaction is instinctual and is controlled by the subconscious mind.

Does it make sense?

No doubt about it!

The Physical Body

The body is nothing but the physical instrument we live in. The actions and behaviour undertaken by the physical body are governed by our habits, values and beliefs which are entirely under the control of the subconscious.

This is similar to the cell phone example, wherein the call being made by the cell phone is entirely under the control of the network provider.

The choices we make and the actions we take ultimately determine the results we achieve.

Does it all add up now?

The understanding of the above concept is critical to the reprogramming of the mind.

Now, the mind is incredible and miraculous, but if you read the above portions carefully, you would have noticed a flaw. And we can use this flaw to our ultimate advantage!

What is the flaw?

The flaw is that the subconscious mind is totally deductive. It cannot differentiate between something that you experience in reality and something that you imagine.

What does this even mean?

It means that the same areas of the brain are activated whether you are actually doing something physically, or only imagining yourself doing it.

For instance, if you are preparing to deliver a speech, you can either deliver it in front of your friends and family or imagine giving the speech in your mind. Both will help you to prepare just as well.

Doesn't make sense, does it?

Let's go deeper then.

Harvard University conducted a research on the human brain where half the subjects knew how to play the piano, while the other half had never played the piano in their entire life. Never Ever!

Now, both the subjects were asked to do a 5-finger exercise (where one simply goes through the motions of playing the keyboard with their fingers). While the subjects who had played the piano did the practice on an actual piano, the non-players were asked to visualise the same 5-finger exercise over and over again. The results were evaluated after 5 days.

Interestingly, the same part of the brain was activated by the subjects who had never touched the piano (the ones who had only visualised themselves doing the 5-finger exercise) as those who had practised the 5-finger exercise on the real piano.

How is that even possible?

It's possible because of the subconscious mind. It cannot differentiate between something that you experience and something that you imagine.

Still not convinced?

Let me try again.

Are you aware that all medical drugs are supposed to undergo a placebo effect test before they are allowed to be sold?

Now you may not know what a placebo effect is. So let me explain.

During World War II, medical camps and tents were set up near the war zones, but the doctors had very limited resources at their disposal to treat injured soldiers.

Dr. Henry Beecher was in charge of one such camp where he was responsible for treating wounded American soldiers. One day, a soldier was brought to his camp from the battlefield. The soldier was injured severely, and he had to be operated on, or he would die.

While proceeding to operate on the soldier, Dr Beecher discovered that he had run out of morphine. The situation was such that without treatment, the soldier would die; and being operated on without a dosage of morphine, the pain alone would probably kill him.

Now, what could he do?

He and his team were desperate to help the soldier. They had an idea!

What happened next was mind-boggling.

They filled the needle with salt and water and told the soldier that they were administering him with morphine, which would help to subside the pain. After being injected with the salt and water solution, the soldier confirmed that the pain had reduced substantially. Dr. Henry Beecher could then operate on him successfully.

After this treatment, Dr. Beecher tried the salt and water treatment on other soldiers (obviously only when morphine wasn't available). And it was amazing to see that more than 50% of the soldiers reported that the salt and water liquid eased and subsided their pain.

Dr. Beecher then coined the term Placebo Effect to describe the same.

Astonishing, isn't it?

The person receiving the placebo believes it's real, and that is enough for the subconscious to send the signal to the brain and make the fake substance work.

So even though it's "fake medicine" with no properties of morphine, it results in a positive outcome.

Science has no explanation whatsoever for the placebo effect, and doctors don't really care how placebo works, as long as placebo works!

Study after study over decades has proved that the placebo effect is real.

If you do have faith in the medicine you're receiving – or you think you're receiving – then absolute miracles can happen. That's the power of the subconscious mind.

The Pharmaceutical companies began exploiting the Placebo effect. They were selling a dud or a substance with no medicinal ingredient in the form of a pill, a liquid, a cream or an injection.

No wonder, there are now regulations that prohibit them from doing so.

Does the above explanation help you conclude that the placebo effect (which somehow tricks the subconscious) is real?

No doubt about it!

The placebo effect is an astonishing phenomenon, but it's not a part of our everyday life. Usually, the placebo effect happens to us unknowingly without any conscious effort.

But the pressing question is, can we use the placebo effect consciously to our advantage?

Can we hack our subconscious to get the desired result?

The answer is an emphatic YES.

For instance, to boost your energy you can pour water or sugar-water in a can of energy drink, and as you believe it to be the real energy drink, you can feel more energetic upon consuming it.

Another instance where you can use the placebo is to curb your food intake. Start to eat your meals from smaller plates. You can make your subconscious mind believe that you're getting a more generous portion without actually eating more. It will in turn help convince yourself that you're getting satiated faster.

To increase your confidence or reduce your stress, you may put some pills in a bottle and label them as 'Super Confidence booster tablets' and 'Stress Reduction tablets' respectively. Your mind will register that they are actual confidence boosters and will keep your confidence levels up.

Now that you understand how to hack the subconscious to make it believe whatever we want to, you may wonder how this can help you realise your Epic Life Vision?

How can it intensify the feeling and take it deep so that it gets amplified and stays with you longer?

How can it become a part of your mind, soul and your psyche?

The answer to that is, through the implementation of the Actors Technique.

Now a logical question that crops up is, what is this Actors technique all about?

BEGIN YOUR A.C.T. BY ACTING

Aristotle (384-322 BC) the great Greek Philosopher said: "To be virtuous you only have to ACT as if you are virtuous."

What did he mean by that?

What he meant was – if you want to be happy, act as if you are happy.

If you want to be creative, act as if you are creative.

If you want to be successful, act as if you are successful.

If you want to be wealthy, act as if you are wealthy.

Simply stated, the Actors Technique suggests that we just act as if we already are whatever we want to be. It was later echoed by William James, an American Philosopher and Psychologist, who first used the phrase 'Act As If' in 1884.

William James said that if you want to be confident, talented, motivated, determined – just Act As If you are already what you want to be. When you Act As If you already have a specific desired quality or skill, your subconscious sets off a chain of events that will help you acquire it.

To be honest, the Actors technique works along the 'Fake it till you make it' logic.

Now, you may think this isn't making any sense. The mind cannot be fooled so easily.

Then I would say, you are underestimating the power of you hacking your mind.

Now, I may go on and on about the power of hacking your mind, but you would only believe it once you experience it. So, Let's do an exercise to see if it works or not.

Let's try to feel happy and joyful at this very moment.

- **Step 1-** Stand tall with your chest and chin up. No slouching, please.
- **Step 2-** Put a big smile on your face. Come on; you can do better than that. Put a huge smile on your face. You can even laugh if you want to.
- **Step 3-** Stretch out your arms as if you're about to give a big bear hug to someone whom you Love.

   (Please continue standing, smiling and stretching your arms for about 2 minutes.)

Now, I am confident; if you did stretch your arms out and kept smiling for 2 minutes, you would have felt the feeling of happiness all through your body in just 3 simple steps.

It worked, but you're still wondering how it worked?

It is simply because your subconscious mind cannot differentiate between what is real and what you imagine.

If you ACT as if you are happy, it accepts the same and it then sends signals to your brain that you are 'HAPPY'. Your brain then responds by releasing the same chemicals (dopamine, oxytocin, serotonin) that it would have released if you were genuinely happy.

Let's take it one step further.

How can we use this same technique to change our identity to live and realise the Epic Life Vision?

If you Act As If you are someone and Think, Behave and Do things the same way they do, your subconscious mind will accept this as your new reality and your new identity.

As we now know, we think and store memories as images. Our self-image is also an image in our subconscious mind. To make any change permanent, we need to use our conscious mind to impress the desired image onto the subconscious mind.

By acting like the person we want to be, we impress the desired image upon the subconscious mind repeatedly and make the change in our identity permanent.

It doesn't happen in one day. It has to be nurtured through repetition until we super-impose the desired self-image on top of the old self-image. Remember the power of repetition we discussed in Potential Story?

Once this new image is formed, a new identity is formed. And you will now act in congruence with your new identity and manifest your desires. This will help you make a lasting change and not let your Epic Life Vision fade or fizzle out.

> 66 *Whatever we plant in our subconscious mind and nourish with repetition and emotion will one day become a reality."*
>
> **– Earl Nightingale**

Think about this for a moment.

What would you do if you happen to have a child who is continuously failing in mathematics? You would try to help him by getting him extra classes and home tuitions.

As a parent, you would ignore all the other things that he may be good at and focus all your attention to mathematics. He still fails miserably.

You may now start to feel that your child is not meant for mathematics. Sadly, that is a half-truth.

To the naked eye, the problem may appear to be in mathematics, but it's not. The root cause of your child not performing well and failing again and again in mathematics is his identity, his self-image.

Due to certain past experiences, past situations and past results, it has been engraved in his self-image and subconscious that he isn't good at mathematics.

Even though the kid is being taught the same thing as other kids, even though you are getting him tuitions and extra classes, his self-image controls him. The self-image won't permit his true potential to come out.

Whenever he thinks of mathematics - an image of agony, suffering and pain crops up in his mind.

Unless you fix this, nothing else will work.

So, how do you fix this?

Every day in the morning and every night before he goes to bed, make him visualise that he is getting excellent grades in mathematics. Make him believe that everyone is proud of him.

Make him act as he would if he got good grades in mathematics. Make him believe that he is getting better every single day.

After 2-3 weeks of visualisation, you will see that his confidence has started to improve. Soon he will show interest in mathematics which will eventually improve his score.

Remember, the hack is always in the subconscious.

I know you have a question in your mind.

If it is as easy as it sounds, then why can't everybody do it?

So, here's the catch. Acting As If isn't as effective if you don't **believe** in yourself and don't **think** you can do what it takes.

Just mere acting won't make the cut.

You have to BELIEVE in yourself. You have to be emotionally involved by thinking, behaving and doing the things that need to be done. You have to fall in love with the vision.

> *There is a difference between WISHING for a thing and being READY to receive it. No one is ready for a thing until he believes he can acquire it. The state of mind must be BELIEF, not mere hope or wish. Open-mindedness is essential for belief."*
>
> *— Napolean Hill.*

I request you to stop right there. Doesn't this sound familiar? Maybe, something called 'The Law of Attraction'.

Wayne Dyer echoed the same sentiment when he said – "You don't attract what you want. You attract what you are. You create your thoughts, your thoughts create your intentions, and your intentions create your reality."

The Actors Technique truly activates and fuels the Law of Attraction. The moment you decide to become one with the vision – physically and emotionally – then and only then do you start the process of truly designing the life you want to live.

As long as you hold the Epic Life image in your mind and keep ACTing As If, the image will affect your movements. It will also dictate what is attracted into your life.

But what if you do not believe in the Law of Attraction?

Does the Actor's technique not make sense for you?

Let's do a small exercise to find out.

Look around the room where you're sitting and pay attention and notice everything RED in the room. Only the colour RED.

Did you do it?

Please do not read further until you've looked around and noticed all the RED in the room!

Did you do it? Only if you did it, please read along. Now that you've looked for everything RED in the room, can you please help me count the number of things you spotted that was BROWN?

How many BROWN coloured things did you notice?

I am confident that if you did the exercise correctly, you didn't spot any BROWN coloured objects. That's because you were so busy looking for RED that you missed all the BROWN colour in the room.

Before you proceed reading, look for all the BROWN coloured things in the room and then read along.

If you did, you would notice that all the BROWN coloured objects would pop out in front of you, without any effort whatsoever.

Why did that happen?

It's because our mind controls our brain.

And whatever the mind instructs, the brain must follow.

Now, when the mind tells your brain, that ONLY RED is IMPORTANT at the moment, the brain focuses on ONLY RED.

By and large, when your mind focuses on RED, the brain only looks for RED and DELETES any other colour that doesn't match its requirement.

When you change focus to BROWN, the brain looks only for BROWN, and then BROWN becomes prominent and pops up in front of you. This is often referred to as the Reticular Activating System (RAS).

But you're probably wondering, how does this relate to the Actors Technique?

When you Act As If you are the person you want to be, you enter a new state of conscious awareness from where you view your world.

Now, your mind tells your brain that it's important to be like this person. Your Reticular Activating System (RAS) now looks for plots, plans, conditions and circumstances which it would have earlier ignored.

The RAS also deletes any other information which is not important and helps to get away from distraction.

Does it all add up for you now?

Fair enough, though there is one more thing that I want to bring to your kind attention.

WILL IT BE EASY?

Do you think it will be easy to behave, speak and do things as you've already achieved what you desire? Would it be easy to ACT AS IF when your current reality is drastically different from your Epic Life vision?

Will it be easy for you to look into the mirror and see yourself as a FIERY LION when you're indeed ONLY a FEEBLE CAT?

It is only logical to think that when you lack financially on the physical level, how can you think, feel and behave like you're wealthy.

Hey listen, do you think that when actors play a part in a movie, they are that part?

Remember this is a mere performance, even though this might turn out to be the best and most important performance of your life.

When you start moving towards the EPIC LIFE VISION and ACT AS IF you are the person you want to be, your mind will not accept it.

It will give you all the logical and practical reasons justifying why you can never do it.

It will make you *believe* you are crazy to even try, but you have to.

Even worse, your family and friends will make fun of you. They will ridicule you even to try. They will say "Who do you think you are acting to be?" But you have to hold your ground. You cannot budge!

Remember, everything that you see around was once imagined in someone's mind.

Everyone including Einstein, the Wright Brothers and Edison were made fun of. When they set out to achieve their dream, they were all ridiculed before they were considered legend. Remember, this is how it's done, and this is how it has always been done. You have to believe that if you can visualise it, you can have it.

66 *Believe, and your belief will create the fact."*
                                    —William James

Also, for how long do you need to ACT before your EPIC LIFE vision becomes a reality?

I'm afraid no one knows how much time it will take for the Epic Life to manifest. We can allocate the time for it to manifest, but we are only second-guessing.

So, don't feel bad if the manifestation does not happen as per your set schedule. Just keep going for it. You need to keep giving yourself time extension.

If you tell yourself a lie often, you're soon going to believe it. The same way the terrorists think they're doing the right thing.

Now, again you must be wondering if there is any guarantee that this will work for sure.

So let me clear your doubt.

Is there a guarantee? NO!

Is there a Possibility? A BIG YES!

Hence, I would urge you to become a possibilitarian.

> " *I challenge you to become a* **possibilitarian***. No matter how dark things seem to be or actually are, raise your sights and see the possibilities — always see them, for they are always there."*
> — ***Norman Vincent Peale***

Always remember, life is unquestionably intelligent. Without a doubt, it will send you the people, conditions, opportunities, resources, enemies, and circumstances required to empower your journey. All you need to do is believe and open up your mind, heart, and brain and be ready to receive it.

The critical thing to remember from this chapter is that acting As if combined with absolute belief has enormous power.

Ask yourself if you are willing to 'Act As if'?

If yes, you must also make yourself aware of the key factor that makes everything fall into place. I believe it is one of the greatest weapons that you can have in your arsenal. Let us now proceed to the next chapter and explore the phenomenal power of...

FOUR

PRODUCTIVITY
The Mechanics Of Manifestation

> 66 *You will never find time for anything. If you want time, you must make it."*
>
> **– Charles Buxton**

As per Hindu mythology, there occurred an Epic Battle (around 3000 B.C.) in the land of Kurukshetra.

Pandavas and Kauravas (two branches of the same family) fought this Epic battle for the throne of Indraprastha and Hastinapur.

To give you a little background, since the Pandavas and Kauravas were Royal Princes, they were trained to master the art of warfare by the great Guru Dronacharya.

Guru Dronacharya was a legendary and illustrious teacher.

As a Guru, one is not supposed to be partial. Still, Guru Dronacharya could not help but favour Arjuna, the third Pandava.

All the other Pandavas and Kauravas were very irritated by this fact that Guru Dronacharya had a favourite.

One day, the Guru decided to show all his students why he favoured Arjuna.

Guru Dronachaya placed a wooden bird on the branch of a tree. He then invited his students, one by one, to aim at and shoot the arrow at nothing but ONLY the eye of the wooden bird.

Before releasing the arrow, they had to answer a simple question.

He first called Yudhisthir to come up and take his stance.

Guru Drona then Asked Yudhisthir, "What can you see?"

Yudhisthir replied, "I can see a wooden bird, the branch, the leaves, the tree and many other birds."

After listening to the answer, Guru Drona ordered him to put the bow down and return to his place.

Next, he called Duryodhana to take his stance to shoot the eye of the wooden bird.

Again, the same question was asked by Guru Drona, "What can you see Duryodhana?"

Duryodhana answered similarly.

All the remaining Pandavas (except Arjuna) and Kauravas who followed were asked the same question after taking their stance to shoot the eye of the wooden bird.

The answers more-or-less revolved around the same – wooden bird, the branch, the leaves, the tree and many other birds. Some of them added that they could also see their teacher, cousins, and other people standing around.

Finally, it was Arjuna's turn.

Arjuna took his stance and Guru Drona Asked, "What do you see Arjuna?"

Arjuna replied, "I can see the eye of the bird."

Dronacharya asked him again "Arjuna, can you not see the tree?"

"No, I can ONLY see the eye of the bird" was the answer.

Guru Dronacharya kept asking Arjuna if he could see the tree, the bark, the leaves, the fruits, his brothers and cousins. He also enquired whether Arjuna could see Guru Drona or not.

Arjuna's answer was always the same: "I can ONLY see the eye of the bird".

Dronacharya had a smile on his face. He finally got the answer he was looking for. He asked Arjuna to release the arrow.

Arjuna did as instructed. The arrow sped through the air and hit the bird's eye.

Why do you think Guru Drona smiled at Arjuna's reply?

Why did he let only Arjun take a shot at the eye of the bird?

You must have got it right.

While all the cousins had failed to separate their goal from the distractions in their path, only Arjuna was able to ignore everything else and focus on the goal, i.e., the eye of the bird.

Let me ask you something.

In your quest to convert your dream of an Epic Life Vision into a reality, are you willing to be Arjuna?

Are you willing to strip away all the distractions that do not lead you anywhere closer to your goal of the Big 5?

Remember, talk is cheap, the action is expensive!

There are many who talk about how they want to change their life, but only a few are willing to do what it takes.

Are you ready to be a doer and not just a thinker and talker?

Are you willing to join the elite club of achievers who obsessively focus their time and energy on the few things that matter?

If the answer is YES, then and only then, can you convert your dreams into reality.

Before you commit, kindly note, you don't just do it for a day, week, or month. You have to make it a part of your lifestyle.

Would it be easy? NO.

Would it be worth it? Definitely yes!

Let me ask you again.

Do you have the AUDACITY to say no to everything else and focus only on the Big 5?

If the answer is a firm yes, then let's dig a little deeper. Let's get tactical on how to turn your dreams into plans and practical systems so that it shows up in your everyday life.

Let's get started with the Mechanics of Manifestation.

THE BIG ELEPHANT IN THE ROOM

Before we proceed, I must congratulate you. You have not only said a well thought of YES to proceed, but, by now, you are also light years ahead of most of the people on the planet.

Unlike you, most haven't taken out the time to look within and find out what they want in life, and why do they even want it!

So, you must be proud of yourself that you are a step closer to living a fulfilling life.

However, there is one key piece still missing from the puzzle.

Any guesses on what that is?

It's the specific action that you must take to make it happen. The action that makes the difference and helps you bridge the gap between goal setting and goal achieving.

That's what makes the difference.

We shall get to that soon, but before we do, we must address a problem that has the potential to kill your Epic Life vision right in its infancy.

I feel like Nostradamus now as I can see the future!

I can see you cursing me after two months. You are going to say "Koonal, everything sounded good – Epic health, Epic relationships, Epic career, Enjoyment and Interior development.

I really wanted to work towards it, but buddy, I HAVE NO TIME!"

Can you see that coming too?

Hey listen, we live a life where we have more demands placed on us than any other time in human history. We live in a world where we are continually being pulled in so many different directions.

I am no fool. I know for a fact that you will have to handle all of life's urgency and demands coming at you first.

Amidst all of that, how do you stick to your Epic Life vision?

When life happens, more often than not, people fall into a pattern of learned helplessness.

That's when they end up saying "I'd like to do it, but I don't have time for it."

As a result, they either give up or end up lowering their expectations from life per se; and some wise ones defer it to doing it later when they think they will have more time.

Can you guess when they will have more time? NEVER!

They lose all the passion, joy and vibrancy they had attached to their vision.

Let's admit it, to achieve anything meaningful; we must address the big elephant in the room first. Or else you will get sucked back into living a life of default vs curating your Epic Life.

Therefore, the first thing we need to do is to find ways to create more time.

That is what we mean by real productivity. Productivity is nothing but having more time for what truly matters to you. It helps you move forward towards your ultimate dream of fulfilling the Epic Life Vision.

So how do you create more time?

At this stage, it would be nice to first understand what time is, and how one should spend time to have a passionate and fulfilling life?

WHAT IS TIME?

Time is nothing but a quantified feeling.

Let me explain this to you.

For a moment I request you to kindly ignore the watch on your wrist, or the clock on the wall, or the one on your cell phone and think about this:

How would you figure out how long something takes, other than by how it feels to you at the moment?

Still Confused?

Let me give you some examples-

Have you ever been stuck in a traffic signal when you were getting late to reach somewhere?

How did you feel at that moment in time?

I'm assuming that like me, you too would have felt that it took an eternity for it to turn Green from Red.

Or, have you ever been in a meeting that was so boring that 1 minute felt like an hour!

I know I have been in that situation, and it felt like time had literally stopped.

When you hate what you are doing, and feel you are out of control, is when time seems to last forever (20 minutes seems like 2 hours).

On the other hand, have you ever been on a date with someone charming or done something that you absolutely love, and time just flew? You were enjoying yourself so much that 2 hours felt like only 20 minutes!

Simply stated, a minute can feel like an eternity when you do NOT like something. On the contrary, time ceases to exist if you're totally involved and genuinely love what you are doing.

Does it make sense now?

A day has 24 hours or 1440 minutes or 86400 seconds. More time is only a state of mind which is achieved when you absolutely love what you are doing, as then, time seems to disappear (2 hours feels like 20 minutes).

Now, what we can learn from people who are fulfilled and live a passionate life is that they spend most of their time doing things they love.

Hence, if we want to be successful and fulfilled, we should learn from them and spend most of our time doing things we love. It's a no brainer.

But, wait a minute.

What if I love playing video games or spending time on social media?

Does spending time on them qualify as living a fulfilled life?

Intriguingly, the question is legitimate, **but the answer, both you and I know, is a big NO!**

As discussed in chapter 2: Purpose, there is a difference between pleasure and enjoyment.

PLEASURE VS ENJOYMENT

Pleasure Activities

Goal

Away From Goal

Enjoyment Activities

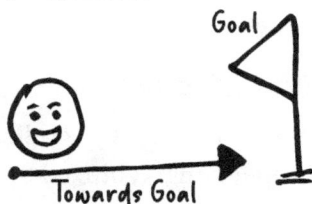

Goal

Towards Goal

By now you would have realised that we need to spend our time doing things we love, but it should be meaningful, i.e. it should help us move the needle towards our Epic Life Vision and help us make it a reality.

To be truly successful and fulfilled, you must spend time being committed to what I call **T.I.M.E., i.e. Totally Immersed in Meaningful Execution.**

We must be totally immersed because when we are not totally immersed in what we are doing, it sends our productivity for a toss. Many of us feel that we can multi-task and our productivity isn't hampered, but there is a ton of research that proves otherwise. **That's the myth of multi-tasking.**

To get more clarity on what's meaningful and what's not let us go more-in-depth. Let's make some distinctions so that we can experience the ultimate joy, passion and fulfilment that we desire and deserve.

WHERE DO YOU SPEND MOST OF YOUR TIME?

(Adapted from Eisenhower's Urgent/Important Principle.)

Where and how we spend our time makes a huge difference not only in the results we achieve in life but also in how we experience the quality of our life. It affects whether you are always stressed or fulfilled.

In our present world filled with demands, the ability to filter the noise, and choose what's meaningful and what's not, is an essential skill to have.

1. Zone of Pleasure

Have you ever mindlessly scrolled through social media, eaten without being hungry, binged on TV shows/news or Netflix, or played video games over and over again?

If you have, then you know what I mean by the zone of pleasure.

Activities in this zone provide instant gratification/pleasure and do not require any attention or mental bandwidth. Whenever we feel bored, lack passion, or are stressed and exhausted, we spend most of our time in this zone.

Though it's fun to spend time in the zone of pleasure, it's a distraction as it takes you AWAY from and not towards your Epic Life Vision.

The bottom line is that activities in this zone are neither important nor urgent. Spending time here will never add any meaning to or enrich your life.

Caveat: *Distractions are things that don't add meaning to your life. Your kids and family are not classified as distractions.*

2. Zone of Fool's Paradise

Have you ever had a busy day where you thought you had gotten a lot done, but at the end of the day you felt like you made no progress whatsoever?

Welcome to the Zone of Fool's Paradise.

Examples include answering numerous phone calls and replying to emails and WhatsApp messages that could have waited. It includes numerous interruptions by colleagues dropping into your office asking for your help or maybe a friend dropping by unannounced during your productive time.

While these tasks may be important to others, they are not necessary for you. These are urgent demands of others around you that derail you from making any significant progress during your day.

People who spend most of their time in this zone often suffer from "Nice-Guy Syndrome" as they want to always please others at the expense of their own happiness.

It's not necessarily bad, but you should maintain a balance, or else you will end up having personal frustration or resentment towards those who steal your time.

You may be amazed that the zone of Fool's Paradise also includes doing tasks to check off from your to-do lists.

Now, you may ask how can checking of to-dos not be important?

At this juncture, **I would like to debunk the myth of to-do lists.**

Most people fill their planners with to-do lists. They feel happy and experience a sense of satisfaction by ticking them off. They never evaluate if it is (in any way) helping them progress towards their goal/dream or anything at all.

For most people, the most important things in life get shoved aside to manage their "to-do" list – the things that are urgent, rather than doing what's important. We somehow feel we have to do them first before even taking care of our own lives.

You may keep ticking things off the to-do list, but if it doesn't help you progress towards the outcome you desire, it means nothing!

One must acknowledge the difference between being busy and being productive.

Please remember activities in this Zone of Fool's Paradise may grab your attention as they seem urgent and important, but in reality, you can avoid it as they are not important at all.

The truth is people who spend most of their time in the Zone of Fool's Paradise are doing precisely what the title implies. They are being happy and satisfied as they think they are doing a lot. They are unaware of the fact that they might be running on a treadmill. They may be busy but are not moving anywhere closer to their goal or accomplishing anything meaningful. It is only a movement which is being confused as an achievement.

3. Zone of Pressure cooker

Do you remember a time when you had only 2 days left to file your taxes or maybe submit a term paper?

How stressed were you?

The Zone of the Pressure Cooker is precisely like that. It is a zone which is usually accompanied by a highly stressful environment, and the major fear is that the pressure within the cooker, if left unattended, might cause it to explode.

The activities in this zone typically consist of crisises, emergencies, problems and deadlines.

Examples include work-emergencies that require immediate fire-fighting, family emergencies that require immediate care (child injuring themselves, a heart attack of a family member). It includes certain emails (job offer, an email for a new business opportunity that requires immediate action), certain household chores, the car having a break-down etc.

These activities are important and require our immediate attention. The salient features of activities in this zone are that they provide us with stress and frustration and no choice or freedom.

The fact of the matter is that life presents these to us on its own, and more often than not, we cannot plan for them in advance.

But beware: sometimes they are a result of our negligence. With a bit of planning and proactiveness, we can reduce the amount of time we end up spending in this zone.

For instance, instead of waiting until the last minute to file our tax returns, we could schedule our time in a way so that we're done with our tax filing a week in advance. Or instead of waiting for the car to break down, we can schedule regular maintenance and servicing.

The trick is to tackle them when they are important and not urgent to avoid unnecessary stress and frustration. Which finally brings us to...

4. Zone of Enjoyment and Flow

Do you remember how your 1-week family holiday seemed to get over as if it was only 2 days?

Time just flew, isn't it?

If you're looking for a life that provides lasting happiness, fulfilment, and success, then you might want to spend most of your time in this zone.

Activities in this zone fulfil us and provide us with happiness in the truest sense.

Examples include spending quality time with family, contemplating what you want from life and planning for the same. It also includes exercising to create energy and charge your body, spending time on a rewarding hobby, reading life-enriching books or getting into spirituality. It even includes strategising about your career.

These activities don't have a pressing deadline. Still, they are instrumental in helping you achieve your Big-5 or realising your Epic Life Vision.

So, when we know these activities are so important, why do we not spend most of our time in this zone?

Psychologists suggest that as human beings, we are designed to have a Present Bias, i.e., to be biased towards urgency.

This implies that we tend to forget what's important and place a lot of importance on urgency.

We tend to give more importance to things that are most pressing at the moment. It's really hard to get motivated to do something when there isn't a deadline looming over our heads.

As the Zone of Enjoyment and Flow activities never seem urgent and never demand our immediate attention, we keep deferring them. We somehow console ourselves by saying "I'll get to those things someday after I have taken care of the urgent stuff". This is what I call the Tyranny of Someday – as this 'someday' will never arrive!

Do you now realise why most people complain that their life isn't moving forward or why there is no juice or fulfilment in their lives?

I know, I know, by now you must be saying, "Koonal, enough of philosophy and theory, let's get into some action now!".

I'll stop now before I start sounding like a spiritual guru.

And let us shift our gear to the Mechanics of Manifestation.

TIME AUDIT
(Keep a Pen/Pencil and Paper handy)

If you want more time, you must first take out some time and think about the way you are living. Reflect upon whether you are living the way you want to live or not.

As such, before we proceed further, it would be wise to reflect on and analyse. Ask yourself, in a typical week, what percentage of time do you spend in each of the 4 zones mentioned above. (The cumulative total should be 100%)?

(Remember we aren't looking for the exact percentage break-up. We are only looking for a rough estimate to get some perspective on where we stand today).

I do not know about you, but people end up spending most of their time in the Zone of the Pressure Cooker and (more often than not) end up living a life of stress.

They then spend a significant part of their balance time in the Zone of Pleasure to move away and de-stress.

If you too are in that category, then you must consciously choose to redesign your life. So that you may spend a higher percentage of your time in the Zone of Enjoyment and Flow, and simultaneously reduce the portion of the time, you spend in other zones.

Am I suggesting you leave everything and spend all of your time in the Zone of Enjoyment and Flow?

Certainly not. Kindly do not get me wrong.

If you only plan for the future and spend time on your hobbies, then life can become boring. Challenges, stress and urgency spice up your life.

I am also not suggesting that we go entirely off the grid and spend no time on social media or never watch Netflix again. We all deserve to indulge in some pleasurable activities and fool around.

If we truly want to enjoy what life has to offer, we need to play in all the 4 zones of our life.

What I am suggesting with all love and respect is to consciously decide the percentage of time you want to spend in each zone.

The Time Audit exercise will help us ascertain what percentage of time we are spending in which zone. We can then consciously decide and design a life where we spend our time as per our conscious choice and not as a default setting.

Ideally, if we want a fulfilled life and play full out in all the zones, we can have an approach of **10/20/30/40** as a place to start with.

> **The zone of pleasure – Spend a maximum of 10% of your time here.**
> **The zone of fool's paradise – Spend a maximum of 20% of your time here.**
> **The zone of pressure cooker – Spend a maximum of 30% of your time here.**
> **The zone of enjoyment and flow – Spend a minimum of 40% of your time here.**

Before you read further, I would request you to take some time out to introspect. Get a reality check of the time you spend in the 4 zones.

Kindly note, if you do not take out time to introspect, and keep on reading, then you may know things intellectually, but it will not help you progress in life.

> *If you let your learning lead to knowledge, you become a fool. If you let your learning lead to action, you become wealthy."*
>
> **— Jim Rohn**

If you did take some time out to do the above exercise, you would feel a sense of joy.

What next?

If you've read and come so far in the book, I am sure you are an achiever.

Most people give up and never commit to taking action that can improve their lives. Only an achiever like you would want to persist and accomplish more incredible feats.

Now, an achiever has some inherent qualities when it comes to time. He:

- Never wastes time (consciously) on things that lead nowhere.
- Never spends more time on anything than it rightfully deserves
- Tries to get more done with minimum effort.

So, the next logical step after you've completed the Time Audit, would be to take out 30-60 minutes of your time and prepare a *Not-To-Do List*.

NOT-TO-DO LIST

What's a not-to-do list?

The Not-to-Do List is a list of activities that suck your time, have low value, drain your energy and do not push you towards your true goals. It's a list of tasks we DECIDE NOT TO DO, no matter what.

> *It's the only thing you can't buy. I mean, I can buy anything I want basically, but I can't buy time."*
>
> **— Billionaire Investor Warren Buffet**

Now, you may ask which task should be on your not-to-do list.

Come on, you know it better than me.

These are tasks that you know you shouldn't be spending any time on. These are activities that:

- Distract you and waste your time
- Stress you out and give you anxiety
- Drain your energy without any meaningful outcome
- You feel obligated to do
- Don't need to be done
- Are other people's responsibility

Some common examples include checking emails, social media and app notifications all the time. It also includes meetings without a clear agenda, gossiping about others, watching the same news for hours etc.

Once you've prepared a not-to-do list, you may incorporate what I call the D.A.T.E Protocol to take your productivity several notches higher.

D.A.T.E. PROTOCOL

So, what's a D.A.T.E Protocol?

D.A.T.E stands for:

D| Delegate
A| Automate
T|Terminate
E| Execute

What I am suggesting is that before doing ANY task, ask yourself these questions.

1) Can it be (D) Delegated to someone else?

Make a note of this: Delegation is one skill that you have to master.

Hey listen, everyone has a million-dollar idea, but not everyone gets the time to execute it because they are so caught up in the day to day operations of their business.

If you can master the art of delegation, you can bring about the most significant shift in the quality of your life. Also, delegation helps by freeing you so that you can spend more time in the Zone of Enjoyment and Flow.

Most business owners, if not all, are business operators. They are playing the role of a CEO and also of a Chief Assistant at the same time. This is costing them a fortune, and this is what restricts exponential growth.

It's counter-productive to be doing something that (1) doesn't matter to you, (2) doesn't lead to your growth, and also (3) that someone else could do for you.

Imagine living a life where you spend time doing only those things that you absolutely love or things that help you grow!

Imagine living a life where you delegate most of the things that you hate to do!

Wouldn't it be fantastic?

Now, you would say that delegation costs money.

Maybe you're in a stage where you are bootstrapped, or perhaps you don't want to spend.

I get it and understand it completely.

Let me quote Billionaire Investor Warren Buffet here: Winners look at value, victims look at the cost.

Can you ascertain the value of your happiness and fulfilment when you are not doing anything you hate or do not like? Can you ascertain the value of your satisfaction where you focus only on things that you are good at and make more money by doing only what you love?

Probably, it's priceless!

Though I understand that maybe you cannot afford it now, it is my earnest request to either be creative and find a way out, or work as hard as you can so that you can afford it soon.

What could be another reason that might stop you from delegating?

You might say, "Koonal, I don't want to delegate because whenever I delegate, I find that the quality of work gets deteriorated. It does not match up to my standards".

In that case, you need to hire the right person for the job, train them and have systems and checks in place to ensure that quality is not compromised and is to your satisfaction.

Kindly remember, delegation is a vital component. It will help you create more time to focus on the Big 5 and realise your Epic Life Vision.

If you fail to delegate, you might simultaneously fail to make your dreams a reality.

2) Can it be (A) Automated so that you don't have to spend more time when the task reoccurs?

Do you tend to find yourself doing little things regularly?

If yes, could you put systems into place instead of repeating those same actions over and over again?

For example, if you travel a lot, could you arrange your clothes so that you don't have to think about it when it's time to pack? Could you pre-stock a toiletries bag that you can simply throw in your suitcase? Or maybe enter your seating and meal preferences in your favourite airline's frequent flyer program?

What about sending cards to your friends and family for special occasions?

There are online services that do it for you. You just pick a design and type a quick message.

Automate your life so that you can spend as much time as you can doing things you love.

3) Is the task required, or can it be (T) Terminated?

This is one of the most powerful questions of the D.A.T.E protocol.

Once you ask yourself if the task needs to be done at all, more often than not, you will end up being at the peak of your productivity. As now, you will only do tasks that are meaningful to you.

4) If I cannot delegate it, automate it or terminate it, do I need to (E) Execute it now or can I defer it for a later date?

If the answer to deferring the task is No, then you must execute it.

The D.A.T.E protocol shall help you save a lot of your time. It shall help you design a life instead of living a life of default. Not only that, it will empower you to stop reacting at whatever comes at you.

And now you shall have time for and do the tasks that truly matter the most to you!

We must carefully audit time, prepare a not-to-do list and follow the D.A.T.E protocol. If we do it well, we will find enough time to work on our Epic Life Vision.

So, the next time you catch yourself saying "I don't have time for designing my life", tell yourself, that's a lie.

Once the excuse of lack of time is out of the equation, we can go all in and play full out.

As of now, we have successfully established the philosophy and strategy of what we need to do to get more time.

But to turn our dreams into reality, we need more than a time management system. We need a life management system – a structure that helps us design and manage our lives to get what we want.

Let us begin the journey to understand and plan how to make the Epic Life happen.

THE BIG 5 AUDIT – THE JOURNEY FROM LIVING A LIFE OF DEFAULT TO LIVING A LIFE OF DESIGN

Adapted from the wheel of life by Paul J Meyers.

Let us take out some time to look at your Big 5. As discussed earlier, these 5 areas are critically important for us to continually focus on and improve upon to have a successful and fulfilling life.

WHEEL OF LIFE

Now think of the Big 5 as spokes of a wheel wherein the centre of the circle is 0% and the outer end of the circle is 100% of what you ultimately desire in that particular facet.

Pick one facet at a time and ask yourself, where am I from 0 to 100% of what I want from my life?

Figure out the percentage and shade the corresponding area.

For example, visualise the image of your Epic Life health. If that is 100%, now, compared to that vision, what percentage would you think you are currently at?

Do you feel you are currently at 10% or are you at 40% compared to where you finally want to be?

If you feel you are at 40%, then shade the area demarcated at 40%.

At this point, you might think, what if I put the mark in the wrong area? Will I ruin this exercise?

I would request you to please relax.

You do not have to have the exact percentage. This is not the end-all and be-all. We are only looking at a ball-park percentage to get some perspective.

There is no right or wrong.

DO NOT GET WORRIED and just do it with a gut-level feeling.

After you are done shading all the areas of the Big 5, you will get a complete and thorough understanding of the shape of your wheel.

Once you've completed the process, take a good look at the wheel of your life and visualise this wheel as if it were a wheel on your car called life.

If you are like most humans, this shape is kind of bizarre at the moment.

That's where your life is at now!

How do you imagine your car to run on a wheel-shaped like the above image?

Imagine your life if you were going at a speed of 10 km/hour with a wheel-shaped like the one above.

I am sure you would imagine it to be a bumpy ride.

But hang on a minute. What if you are an achiever who wants speed and momentum in life and you were going at a speed of 120 km/hr, what would it look like then?

I am sure you could imagine that it would land you into an accident.

Take a moment to ponder; why does your wheel look so bizarre?

The answer is simple yet profound.

Most of us live a life of reaction where we focus our time, energy, and resources either on things that require immediate attention or because we enjoy doing them.

As a result, areas on which we focus our time, energy, and resources grow while other facets get ignored.

Please beware! At the moment, it might seem okay, but these ignored facets might later come and bite us. We do not want that, do we?

For example, if we focus a lot on our career and ignore our health, later it might come back to us as a disease. And the disease will not allow us to make any advancement in our career.

In a nutshell, as an achiever who wants a life of success and fulfilment, you must ensure that the "wheel" is as Round (even shading in all facets) and as Big (closer to 100%) as possible.

You must ensure that you create habits and plans that enable all the facets to grow together. That's when the quality of life begins to change, and that's how you start to design your life.

Now the impending question is, how do we do it?

To make it round and big, we need to ensure that we spend sufficient time, energy and resources on all the 5 facets that matter the most to us.

To do this, let us begin the process of creating your Epic life plan – A plan which enables you to create balance, momentum and power. A plan that helps us to bridge the gap between where we are and where we ultimately want to be.

THE TOP-DOWN APPROACH TO PLANNING

What's the best way to plan your journey from where you are on the wheel of life, to where you ultimately want to be?

How do you take yourself from the very big picture of what you ultimately want and break it down into small tasks that you can do every single day? How can you 'make it happen' and produce the results you are after?

Most people plan in a traditional way, i.e., using the bottom-up approach, which simply focuses on scheduling your non-prioritised to-dos and checking them off.

The problem with planning with a bottom-up approach is that it lacks having a focus on the big picture. It leaves us dissatisfied, because even after having a busy day, we may hardly move forward in life.

Most leaders and iconic producers begin with the end in mind and have a Top-Down Approach.

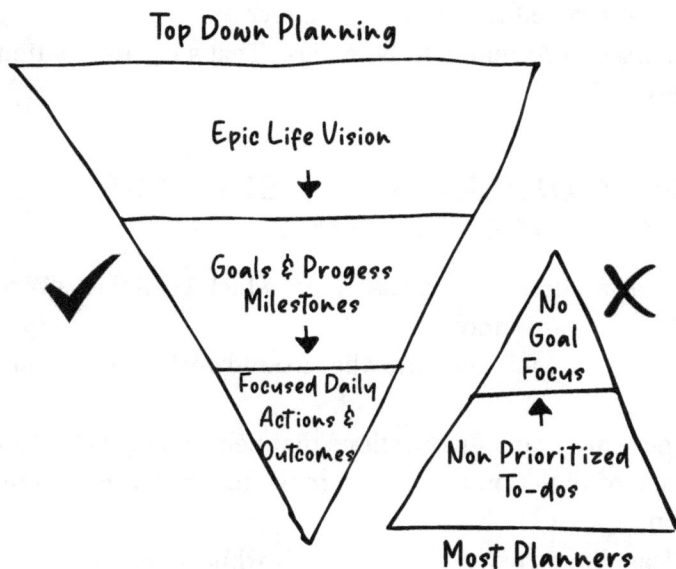

Top Down Planning

Epic Life Vision
↓

Goals & Progress Milestones
↓

Focused Daily Actions & Outcomes

✓

No Goal Focus

↑

Non Prioritized To-dos

✗

Most Planners

A Top-Down Approach looks at planning from a better vantage point, i.e., the top, which focuses on what you want (Ultimate Life Vision) and why you want it.

That's how we will do it too.

We now know the 5 areas of our life that are most important, we also have a vision of what we ultimately want from those 5 areas of our life. To top it all, we also have an empowering and compelling 'why'.

You now need to look more in-depth into specific outcomes you want for each of these 5 areas and plan what you want to achieve in a year. You then deconstruct the year into what you will achieve in the next quarter, which will make it easy for you to decide what you want to do every week, and then on a daily basis.

In essence, the top-down approach creates an effortless focus on outcomes which align with your goals and provide you with fulfilment, happiness and success daily.

But how do we know what we need to plan on a weekly basis so that we can efficiently execute daily?

The secret to that is to be Aware. That's the foundation of success.

THE FOUNDATION OF SUCCESS: #5W AWARENESS TOOL

To get awareness, we shall use a tool which I call the #5W tool.

What is a #5W tool?

#5W is a tool that lays the groundwork/foundation for success.

These are a set of 5 questions that helps you get clarity and a sense of direction on how to move towards your Epic Life Vision.

Please have a pen and paper handy while doing this exercise.

We need to do the 5W exercise for each area of the Big 5 separately.

Let's get started.

Where

Where are you right now?

Once you have completed the Big 5 audit, you can now take each facet and start breaking it down.

At first, you must start from where you are right now.

Imagine you are sitting in a car, and you have to go somewhere. You have put the desired location in the GPS (Global Positioning System).

For the GPS to take you from where you are to where you want to be, the first thing that needs to be put in the GPS for it to work efficiently is your current location or the starting point.

Similarly, to reach our Epic Vision's desired location, we must first be aware of our current location or our starting point.

Once we know where we are and face our moment of truth, it becomes easier to navigate in the desired direction. All change must start with honesty.

Maybe you're not happy with the way the relationship is shaping up.

Maybe you're not happy with the way your company is growing or the income you have.

Maybe you're not happy with the job you're in.

Maybe you're in a terrible shape with your health because of all the junk food you're having.

You could be feeling some pain, or you could be feeling uncomfortable in certain areas of The Big Five of your Epic Life.

Interestingly, research proves that human beings are designed to do more in their life to avoid pain than to get pleasure.

It's time we acknowledge the pain in our lives and expose ourselves to it. It's time to feel the pain. It's time we call a spade a spade. The pain has the power to motivate you. It has the power to push you.

It can help you gain massive momentum.

The real question to which we seek the answer is, 'What habits, beliefs, and behaviours have led you to this place?'.

Key points to note: We are just acknowledging and reflecting. We don't have to stay in the rabbit hole and keep feeling sad.

Be honest to yourself. The more open you are about where you are, the clearer will your path/journey be.

Why

Why is it an absolute must for me to get success in this aspect of my life?

Describe in detail, why you want it.

Why will you do whatever it takes to make your dream in this area a reality?

As discussed in Chapter 2 - Purpose, a big and compelling vision won't stand pace without an even more powerful and compelling reason for you to achieve it.

If you do not have a compelling reason to achieve the Epic Life Vision, you will let go of it when things are not going as per plan. Without a compelling reason, you might say 'let it be, life is good as it is.'

Let's not forget, when you encounter failures and rejections, only a strong and compelling WHY, will give you the strength to follow through.

Who

Who could help you reach where you want to go?

Who could be a mentor or a coach for you in this area?

Is there anyone who has achieved what you want in this facet? Try to model his habits, beliefs and strategies.

Who could help you be more accountable to your commitments so that you follow through?

Are there any other resources or tools you have to make this happen? For instance, books, videos on YouTube, seminars etc.

What

66 *We cannot become what we want to be by remaining what we are."*

— *Max DePree*

Is there a reason why you are where you are?

Ofcourse yes!

Almost inevitably, we are where we are in our life because of our current paradigms, knowledge, skills, habits, attitude and environment.

Think about it. You often update and upgrade your cell phone, but how often do you upgrade and update yourself in terms of knowledge, skills, habits, attitude and environment.

It would be best if you had a U.P. (Upgrade Protocol) to up your game. You need to consciously and continuously update and upgrade yourself the same way you update and upgrade your cell phone.

You need to ask yourself continually:

- What specific new skills might I need to get there?
- What daily rituals must I have so that I develop a sense of discipline to follow through?

When

When will you achieve them?

This is how you deconstruct the Epic Life Vision from aspirational to achievable.

66 *Think of a car driving through the night. The head-lights only go a hundred to two hundred feet forward, and you can make it all the way from California to New York driving through the dark because all you have to see is the next two hundred feet.*

That's how life tends to unfold before us.

If we just trust that the next two hundred feet will unfold after that, and the next two hundred feet will unfold after that, your life will keep unfolding, and it will eventually get you to the destination of whatever it is you truly want, because you want it."

—Jack Canfield

When you put your desired destination on the GPS, it breaks down the entire journey into points. It says go from point A to B, B to C, C to D and so on until you reach your final destination.

Similarly, our Epic Life is a destination in itself; we need to break down our journey and plot our course. We need to make the aspirational life's vision achievable by figuring out what we need to do between where we are and where we want to go.

We need to deconstruct the dream into SMART (Specific, Measurable, Achievable, Relevant and Time-Bound) Goals.

It might seem like a daunting task, but all we need to do is have faith and take the first step.

66 *Take the First Step in Faith. You Don't Have to See the Whole Staircase, Just Take the First Step."*

—Martin Luther King, Jr.

Ask yourself, "What are the Key Focus Areas that I need to achieve to get my Ultimate Result?"

List the 3-5 key focus areas that are absolutely necessary to significantly impact your Epic Life Vision.

These key focus areas should be the building blocks of your ultimate vision. They should help you make significant progress in your pursuit.

Ask yourself: Over the next 1 year, what do I need to achieve to make this the single most incredible year in terms of my health, career, relationships, wealth and interior architecture?

After you've laid your 1-year vision, ask yourself what can I achieve in the next 90 days?

It would be best to make it as specific as possible and not keep it vague or open-ended.

For instance, if your goal is to have a successful e-commerce business, and you want to reach out to investors for funds to expand the business further, then you can break that down as follows:

In the next 1 year:
Have over 1000 satisfied clients and get them to market for me by word of mouth.
In the next 90 days:
Reach out to 100-200 potential new clients every month through social media marketing strategies to have 1000 satisfied clients by the end of 1 year.

Guess what? You will look at those 1-year plans and 90-day outcomes and decide what you want to do this month. The monthly outcome plan will help you to determine what you're going after this week and ultimately decide on what outcome you will go for on a daily basis.

This is how you ultimately design the life you deserve.

You can repeat the same exercise for all The Big 5's.

Once we break down the entire journey, it starts to look more achievable instead of daunting.

It gives you a feeling that you can do it.

Remember – you are just guessing the timeline. You may or may achieve it within the desired timeframe. But at least you now have a roadmap that will guide you.

Does it make sense?

This is how you start with a vision and bring it all the way down to a real plan where the rubber meets the road.

If it's the first time you are doing it, it will need a bit of tweaking here and there.

None of us is good or perfect at it.

Like anything in life, the more we do something, the better we get at doing it.

After you've done this, you need to begin applying these principles to create your Weekly Plan and act on them daily to get the results that you ultimately desire.

But how can we design a great weekly plan that helps us act effectively daily?

THE WEEKLY PLANNING PROTOCOL: WHERE IT ALL COMES TO PLAY

The Weekly planning protocol is where you can see how everything fits together. It is here that all of the above philosophy comes together in a simple, practical plan.

It is the weekly planning protocol that helps you put the focus back on the Big 5. It enables you to get rid of stress by providing clarity. It helps you design a doable yet super powerful plan so that you can build massive momentum by taking one small step at a time.

All in all, the weekly planning protocol is a tool that helps you take your Epic Life Vision, dreams and goals and translate them into achievable weekly and daily outcomes.

Please note it is not a software, it's only a thinking guideline.

We need to take out 60-90 minutes of our time every week and get in touch with our Life Vision and then align our weekly plans to it.

The fundamentals of an excellent weekly planning process are what I call being in **F.L.O.W.**

- **F| Focus:**

  Focus on things that matter the most, i.e., your Epic Life Vision (the Big 5) and the compelling 'Why'.

  Now we know why the 'Why' is the most important, don't we?

  Think and reflect upon the dream of your Epic Life Vision. Connect with the vision and fall in love with it through the power of weekly repetition.

  Remind yourself of the compelling 'why' so that you follow through no matter what!

- **L| List:**

  List your achievements from last week and celebrate every small win. List what's going right in your life.

  It is very easy to get demotivated and lose sight of your Epic Life Vision. Listing your small wins helps you be positive and stay motivated.

  Researchers have found that if you record the good things that happen to you at the end of the week, you create massive momentum. Your brain releases dopamine – the feel-good hormone when you recall the good stuff. So it helps you feel good even if you've had a tough week.

  List the outcomes you couldn't achieve and ponder why it didn't happen.

  List and measure your progress.

  Remember, you cannot manage something you don't measure. Most people don't follow through on their goals because they measure their progress once in 6 months or a year. If you measure it weekly, research says you have a 300% higher chance of following through and achieving your goal.

- **O| Outcome optimisation:**

You optimise your coming week by capturing and scheduling the Big 5 Outcomes for next week.

How do you decide your Big 5 Outcomes for next week?

Simple. You must look at the 5 areas of your Ultimate Vision to stimulate your thinking. You must then contemplate and come up with 1 achievable outcome from each area of the Big 5 in your weekly plan.

Follow the D.A.T.E protocol and prioritise the action steps/outcome that you must accomplish the next week.

- **W| Win Freeze Protocol**

Win Freeze Protocol is the act of committing to an outcome that you will accomplish next week, no matter what.

This is your mission for the next week. If you could achieve this one outcome, you would call your entire week a success.

Think about this for a moment. If you successfully freeze wins every week, you would have at least 50 wins that take you closer to the Epic Life Vision at the end of the year.

Does it make sense?

If you plan your week with F.L.O.W, you can be rest assured that you would have successfully prepared for a great week ahead.

Kindly Remember, planning helps you but isn't everything by itself. You need to act on the weekly plan on a daily basis.

That's the real thing!

The Ultimate Advantage Pro-Tip:

- Make the weekly planning a must. Fix a day and time to do it every week like Saturday at 6 PM or Sunday at 6:00 AM.
- Make sure you are in a peak state and distraction-free while planning your week. As a bonus, you may have some inspiring music playing in the background.
- BONUS: Allot 2 days free for yourself so you can spend some good time in the Zone of Enjoyment.

The crucial take away from this chapter is that productivity is the mechanics required for us to play the big game. It helps us learn a new way to play the game of life. It helps us to respond to demands not by reacting to them but through the conscious direction. It puts you back in control with a sense of certainty and power.

Now, inspite of the demands that life brings to you, you would be able to proclaim that you are running the show. You won't be reacting to all the things around you and wonder why you are not fulfilled anymore.

At the end, an Epic Quality of life is achieved by being productive and deciding to:

Live:

Choosing to 'live' life to the fullest by squeezing every ounce of juice from what life has to offer.

Love:

Choosing to 'love' and share deep, meaningful relationships with people whom you genuinely care about.

Moments that matter

Choosing 'moments that matter' where you spend most of your time doing things that you love. It helps you maintain focus on things that matter instead of being attracted to every shiny object that draws your attention.

Remember, there is always a choice.

What would you choose?

No matter what you decide to choose, there is 'something' without which you cannot achieve or manifest anything!

Read the next chapter to decode what that 'something' really is and how you can have an abundance of that 'something' to rock the boat you would be sailing on. It's time to master the...

FIVE

POWER STATE
The X-Factor Of Peak Performers

> *A man doesn't need brilliance or genius; all he needs is energy."*
>
> **—Albert M. Greenfield**

Beep...Beep...Beep....

It's 7 A.M., and Rahul's alarm starts to ring!

He reluctantly gets up and hits the snooze button on the alarm, and goes back to sleep.

Finally, after snoozing the alarm for at least 3 times, he somehow manages to get up. But he is still not bursting with energy and feels a little exhausted.

First things first, still lazying in bed, he grabs his phone and starts scrolling his social media or news to check out the latest feed. He then checks if he has received any important business emails.

Before we proceed, let me give you some more information about Rahul.

Rahul, aged 45, is a business owner. He met his wife Nisha during college, and they have been together since then. Nisha is a high-ranking bank official.

They have been married for 18 years, and now have two kids – 15-year-old Abhilasha and 11-year-old Rohan. They live in a metropolitan city of India.

Both Rahul and Nisha have demanding careers and add to that the responsibility of raising two kids, who have their busy life schedules as well. Life was as full as it could be.

Now back to Rahul's day.

After taking a bath, he has a rushed breakfast and leaves for office. During the 1-hour commute to work, he is either reading the newspaper or scrolling through social media.

As soon as he reaches the office, he starts fire-fighting the day to day operational problems.

Most of his time is spent in communication (phones, emails and answering to Whatsapp messages), coordinating and following up with his employees. Whenever he sits to get anything meaningful done, he is interrupted by his employees to solve or discuss trivial issues. As a consequence, he cannot concentrate or focus on a single task for long.

He has meetings after meetings (and they all get stretched without reaching any proper conclusion or actionable steps). By the end of the day, he is even more exhausted.

While at work, there is no fixed time for him to have lunch. Depending on his work schedule, he sometimes sneaks in lunch at 2:30 P.M. and sometimes at 4:00 P.M. On some days he skips lunch altogether.

On most days after around 4 P.M., he can sense his energy level fading. It results in decreased levels of productivity and focus, with a simultaneous increase in irritability.

Around 7:30 P.M. he realises it's time for him to leave for home, but his work isn't finished yet. Even though he didn't waste any substantial amount of time sitting idle during the day, he felt that he wasn't at his peak performance all the time, especially during the second half of the day. In fact, a task that should ideally take an hour for him to complete, took him three!

During the 1-hour commute home, he spends time on his phone, either returning calls or answering emails. Sometimes he mindlessly scrolls through social media just to escape all the pressure from the demands of the day.

And one more thing.

He always plans to exercise after work, but that seldom happens as he can find neither time nor the energy to work out. By the time he returns from work, he is exhausted, and the last thing he wants to do is go to the gym or go for a run/cycle.

While having dinner, instead of spending time with his wife and kids, he dines while binging on Netflix or the news till around midnight. Please note, it's not because he doesn't love his family but because he has no energy left to spend time with them. His mind is filled with stress, and he gets solace by getting lost in his television.

This seems to be an endless loop, and every day he keeps feeling even more sluggish and exhausted.

He is always stressed out, overworked, and has no energy or desire to accomplish anything. He is impatient and cynical. All he wants is to get through the day somehow.

But you know what, he wasn't always like this.

Rahul was a man with big dreams and was blessed with the corresponding talent to achieve them.

He was a charmer and always full of life. During his school and college days, he was the star of all social gatherings with his funny jokes and friendly banter.

He took good care of his health through proper nutrition and would work out at least 4 days a week. He was healthy and fit.

It's so unlike today, where his humour is always sarcastic, and he is borderline obese with his belly peeking out over his belt.

When he started his business, he was full of zeal and passion. Every day he worked towards his dreams. He kept going at it relentlessly. As his vision was compelling, he never really took any breaks.

Please take a moment to think about Rahul.

What happened to the man who was so full of life?

What happened to the man who had big dreams and was motivated to achieve them?

What forced him to change?

Perhaps, the answer is simple.

With every passing day, the demands from Rahul's life kept on increasing.

But the power and capacity, i.e., the energy required to meet the demands did not simultaneously increase with the rise in demand.

Most importantly, even though he had potential, he had no energy to manifest his potential.

He was running on empty!

Before you proceed, ask yourself how much of your day-to-day experiences match and resonate with Rahul?

Are you running on empty too?

Do you also feel that you have very little energy/passion?

Do you feel tired and/or exhausted most of the time?

If the answer to the above questions is '*yes*', and if you want to transform and turbocharge your energy and bring out your A-game each day, you are going to find this chapter incredibly valuable.

THE X-FACTOR OF PEAK PERFORMERS

Who comes to your mind when you think of the words: Power and Energy?

Almost always, we associate these words with athletes, construction workers, labourers, farmers etc.

We assume that people who have a desk job don't really need power or energy, as their performance is exclusively dependent on how their brain functions and certainly not by how their body performs.

Nothing could be farther from the truth!

Let me give you some scenarios to ponder upon.

- Have you ever been in a meeting that lasted for 3 or 4 hours? If you have, please visualise what it was like. Was your energy level constant throughout the session, or did you feel that the energy level dropped and you struggled to stay focused after about 1.5 hours?
- Have you ever had a busy day where you were spot on for the first half of the day but by 3 or 4 P.M. you turned impatient and irritable?
- Have you ever had a day when you reached home after work, and you were consumed and distracted by thoughts about your day at work? You were physically present with your family, but mentally you were somewhere else?

Why does it happen?

Here is the answer: Everything in life that matters—from interacting with colleagues and making important decisions to spending time with family— requires an expenditure of energy. Even thoughts, emotions and our behaviours require energy.

As obvious as it may seem, we often tend to ignore the importance of energy at work and our personal lives.

Many people know what they want, and what to do to get what they want, but they do not do it simply because they don't feel like doing it.

The world is filled with geniuses who have talent and skills but do not achieve anything because they do not have the energy required to execute upon their magnificent dreams.

Their mind wants to conquer the world, but they can't even get themselves out of bed!

It's a classic example of the phrase from the Bible which says "the spirit indeed is willing, but the flesh is weak." A modern-day equivalent means, 'I would if I could, but I can't so I shan't'.

Hey look: The Epic Life Vision is a dream, and dreams have the power to make you passionate.

Being passionate is a good start, but it doesn't get you anywhere. You need the energy to move from Point A to Point B.

People who accomplish their dreams or achieve anything substantial in life are not only dedicated, disciplined, determined and desperate; but are also the ones who have the corresponding energy to follow through, no matter what.

Simply stated, passion without energy is like a rocket without high octane jet fuel. You may have the potential and the opportunities to touch the sky, but you will barely leave the ground!

Remember, without the right quantity and quality of energy; you are compromised in any activity you wish to perform.

Therefore, you need to have a deep reservoir and abundance of energy if you want to turn your epic life vision into reality.

Only with an abundance of energy can you have the fire and emotional gas fuel to bring your A-game and meet the increasing demands from things around you.

IS MORE REALLY MORE?

Today, we live in a society where there are more demands for our time than at any other time in history.

So, how do high-performers respond to the increasing demands?

As high-performers are hard-wired with a *do-more* mindset, they tend to respond to demands by working longer hours.

They try to make up by compensating with too little sleep, make do with fast food and being on the run with workplace demands 24/7.

Most return home after a long day at work, feeling completely exhausted.

Let's admit it, instead of experiencing family time as a source of joy and renewal, most of us end up treating it as another demand from life.

We tend to cut corners in our relationships and with our kids because there's no measurable impact from another hour spent with the family. But we assume that another hour at the office could have a significant impact on our business.

As we live in a world with a scarcity of time, we somehow convince ourselves that we have no choice but to fill our day with as many tasks as possible.

We end up working like machines.

Now I'm going to stop you right there and ask you: Are we machines?

You're dead right; we are not.

Working like machines might not seem to have any profound effect in the short run, but over time it inevitably takes a toll on us physically, mentally and emotionally.

When we keep pushing harder and harder, the level of engagement goes down, and we are often tired and frustrated. We reach a tipping point where we begin to become short-tempered and distracted.

Before we realise, we reach a stage where we completely break-down and eventually burn-out. We lose our passion and end up letting go of our dreams. That is when people begin to settle for whatever life has to offer.

Isn't that what happened to Rahul?

Think about this for a moment, what if the way most people live and work in our society is primitive and outdated?

The idea of working longer and harder to get more done might have worked in the industrial age where the workers would produce more output by putting in more hours, but not anymore.

We need to acknowledge and incorporate a new paradigm that works for the new era.

As today, epic producers are not evaluated based upon the length of time they put in, but are rewarded by the creativity and genius they put out in the hours they work.

At this point, we need to ask ourselves - what's more important, (1) the number of hours we put in or (2) the quality of brilliance we bring into the number of hours we work?

If you dive deep, you will realise that determining how productive you are has never been about how many hours you put in. Instead, it's always been about how much of your energy you can invest during the hours you work.

60 hours of energy-focused work beats 80 hours of energy-drained work every single time.

If we can master this one profound concept, we shall discover the secret to not only be more effective but also be much happier.

Please don't get me wrong. I am not suggesting that the quantity of hours you put in isn't important.

I do not know of anyone who achieved substantial success without putting in the hours.

But one thing's for sure, quantity in the absence of appropriate energy in the hours you put in is like a hollow victory. You do not fire with all that you have. You end up compromising efficiency, creativity, innovation and mastery!

The number of hours in a day is fixed, but the quantity and quality of energy available to us are not. Do you now realise why energy is our most precious resource?

Tony Schwartz, the founder and CEO of The Energy Project, has done a lot of research on this.

The Energy project helps individuals (including top-performing athletes and celebrities) and organisations to manage their energy skilfully. It empowers them with energy so that they not only survive but also thrive in a world of ever-increasing demands and complexities.

The Energy project suggests that the most outstanding business owners, artists, and creative producers believe in cycles of periodisation, i.e., managing work and rest ratios.

They understand that in the long run, renewal of energy is as vital as expenditure of energy to be effective at whatever we do.

The epic performers do not want to be running on empty, do you?

Probably not.

THE RHYTHM OF LIFE

Have you ever taken the time to look around and notice the nuances of nature?

If you do, you would see a pattern: a rhythm of activity and rest.

This pattern is evident from the rising and setting of the sun to the ebb and flow of tides, and also in the transition between seasons. Similarly, there exists a rhythmic pattern that we can observe in birds that migrate, bears that hibernate, and animals that nest at predictable time intervals.

Likewise, we humans too have a rhythm like pattern.

Picture this – there is rhythm in the ups and downs of our blood pressure, the way we breathe, our brain waves, heart rate, body temperature etc.

Interestingly, the cycle of ups and downs is what life thrives on – a straight/flat line on the ECG machine signifies that one is dead.

Life   Death

Like everything else in nature, human beings too, are inherently designed to oscillate between activity and rest.

Thus, if we continue to work relentlessly without resting, we defy the basic fabric of nature.

Bottom line: to align ourselves with the laws of nature, we must learn how these internal rhythms operate and how to spend and renew energy.

By understanding this, we can learn to use them to our advantage.

Surprisingly enough, it's never the intensity of expenditure that causes us to break-down, but the duration of expenditure without recovery.

What does expenditure without recovery mean?

It simply means working for extremely long hours without taking rest, working 24/7 without proper sleep, working all year-round without taking holidays etc.

The more you spend energy in a focused and intense way, and then offset it with deep renewal, the healthier, more powerful, and more effective you become.

Healthy patterns of activity and rest lie at the heart of our capacity for full engagement, maximum performance, and sustained health.

Imagine how life would be if you could operate at your Peak Performance, every single moment of your life!? Wouldn't you be able to squeeze out every ounce of juice that life has to offer?

THE TRILOGY OF POWER STATE

The power state of peak energy is what best serves peak performance.

To achieve power state, we must first understand that it is not one-dimensional.

TRILOGY OF POWER STATE

To optimise ourselves, we need to master the 3-dimensional trilogy that commands our energy, i.e., Physical, Emotional and Mental energy, and consciously direct it towards our purpose.

To perform at our best, we need to master all the 3 dimensions. They are interconnected and profoundly influence each other. If you remove any one from the equation, you substantially reduce your ability to unleash the best version of yourself.

Physical Energy

The first component in the trilogy and also the fundamental source on which the trilogy rests is your physical energy. It's the primary source that commands your vitality and provides fuel to the Epic Life mission that you are on.

All legendary performers and achievers fortified their physical energy. They were aware that physical energy is responsible for turbocharging their alertness, enhancing their concentration and amplifying their creativity.

How can we have a deep reservoir of physical energy?

Essentially, if we want to top-up the reservoir of physical energy we must focus on our (1) patterns of nutrition (the food we consume and timing of the same), (2) sleep (quantity and quality), (3)hydration (intake of water), (4) breathing, (5) recouping during the day and last but not least, (6) the amount we move (our level of fitness).

Emotional Energy

Back in 1908, Psychologist Yerkes and Dodson conducted a strange experiment and derived terrific insights. They discovered that if you left rats to race in a maze, they wouldn't care. However, if you gave them mild electric shocks, they would be motivated to complete the race.

But, only up to a certain point.

If you overly shocked them, their performance level would decrease, and they would try to escape the maze and not complete it.

Why am I telling you this, knowing very well that you have no inclination about knowing what motivates rats?

If we set aside the testing on rats, this experiment unearthed two key learnings elucidated below:

1. Rats found a sense of challenge and adventure when they were given mild electric shocks. They moved from a state of inertia to a state of optimal performance. Hence, there seemed to be a relation between emotional charge and performance.

Needless to say, to perform at your best, you need to access a pleasant and positive emotional charge—emotions such as purpose, enjoyment, challenge, adventure and opportunity.

2. The rats' performance level started to decrease when the number of shocks increased. Later, when they couldn't handle the stress anymore, they almost gave up and tried to escape.

As such, an overdose of challenge can lead to a tipping point, when negative emotions of fear, frustration, anger and sadness lead to stress and anxiety.

For our understanding of peak performance, emotional energy is to be managed skillfully to fuel our performance. But we must be cautious not to reach a tipping point where we want to escape and start to live a life of compromise.

Essentially, if we want to boost the pool of emotional energy, we must focus on our patterns of (1) enjoyment (distressing activities) and (2) relationships (people we spend time with).

Mental Energy

Have you ever been present somewhere physically but absent mentally?

Have you ever been so consumed by the thoughts in your head that you couldn't taste the food you were eating?

I know I have.

Nothing is as detrimental to power state as when your mental energy – i.e., the focus is diverted.

Many people who achieved exponential success weren't hard-wired with genius. Still, they could do incredible things because they could harness their mental energy, and monomaniacally focus attention on the few things that truly mattered.

To perform at our best, we need to flex our mental muscle. We need to free our mind from the baggage of the past and the anxiety of the future. We must concentrate on the task at hand.

But, how do you keep away from the negative chatter that keeps on happening in and around you? How do you monomaniacally focus on the task at hand?

It's common to hear well-intended advice like "Be positive" and "Just don't think negative thoughts".

But to me, it seems counter-intuitive.

I sometimes wonder, barring me, is everyone else positive?

How can I pretend that the world is all about rainbows and sunshine when I can feel that isn't the case?

I kept wondering until I came across tons of research that clarifies the same.

According to the Cleveland Clinic, the average person has 60000 thoughts per day. Out of the 60,000 thoughts, over 80% of thoughts are negative!

We can safely say that our brain isn't a part of the "think happy be happy" club.

The fact of the matter is we cannot remove the negative chatter in our head. But what we can do is increase our appetite for 'Realistic Optimism'.

What does realistic optimism even mean?

It's a **realistic thought process** that accepts that the world isn't rosy (filled with rainbows and sunshine), and despite knowing that it isn't, we continue to work towards what we desire.

If we want to develop and flex the muscle of mental energy, we must focus on our patterns of (1) breathing (yoga), (2)visualisation and (3)meditation, and (4)positive self-talk.

As the name trilogy suggests – the three dimensions are related and rely upon each other.

Take a moment to ponder. Wouldn't fatigue and lethargy due to lack of proper sleep make it more challenging to focus and concentrate on the task at hand?

You bet it would—no doubt about it.

Suppose you are feeling stressed and anxious on an emotional level. In that case, it will interfere with your focus and draw energy away from your goals.

Since each system is interconnected, even when one of the three gets depleted, our entire being feels the difference.

We may experience physical lethargy, mental fog and/or emotional fatigue until we restore our energy through holistic, energy-increasing strategies.

Reality Check

(Adapted from energy audit by Tony Schwartz)

Now I may go on and on about the importance of energy but for you to believe and experience it, let us do an energy audit for you.

Please mark whether the following statements are true or false for you.

I regularly get at least 7-8 hours of sleep a day, and I always wake up feeling full of energy and vitality.	
I eat all my meals on time and ensure that I get proper nutrition during the day.	
I consciously take out time during the day to rest so that I can recoup and recharge to be able to perform at my peak levels consistently.	
I understand the importance of water and consciously intake at least 2-3 litres of water to keep myself hydrated throughout the day.	

I regularly move and/or work out to train myself through strength training, cardiovascular exercises, or stretching.	
I am happy and friendly to others at my work.	
I periodically take out time to enjoy my hobbies and/or take vacations.	
I manage to spend enough time with my family and loved ones by being genuinely present, i.e., physically and mentally.	
I can focus on one thing at a time instead of being in a mindless loop of distraction.	
I live each day with a sense of purpose, joy and fulfilment.	

Now, True being 1 and False being 0, calculate your overall score.

What's your score?

____ out of 10

Would you want to score a perfect 10 as now you know that energy is not only the basis of existence but also the primary fuel that enables you to live a fulfilling life that you deserve?

If yes, let us go more in-depth and understand a comprehensive strategy that empowers us to have physical alertness, mental clarity, and emotional composure.

Let us deconstruct a natural, viable and doable framework that helps us reach our power state without the hassle. I call this framework **'The Pyramid of Vitality'**.

The Pyramid of Vitality – helps renewal and in-turn unlocks peak energy by creating an overall healthy lifestyle that allows us to accomplish all we need to do in a day.

PYRAMID OF VITALITY

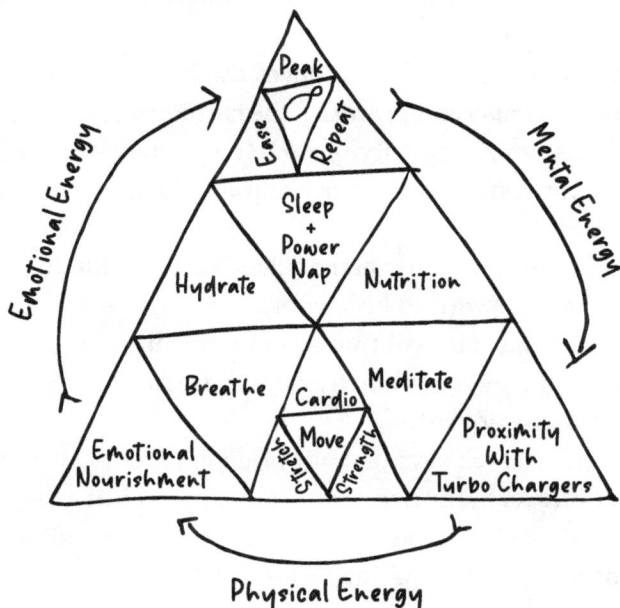

I. Sleep

What's the first thing you compromise on when you are trying to meet the increasing demands of life?

For most, reducing their sleep always seems like a logical solution.

But the bitter reality is that it's not working to your advantage. Lack of sleep is why most people are wiped out. They are neither fully energised nor fully engaged.

Most of us never consciously make time for sleep.

Now, you might say, "Koonal, you don't know how busy my life is. I have kids, I have a business/job, I have a spouse and so many responsibilities to cater to. And not only that, I have so many more things to do!".

I get it, but you have to make time for sleep.

The quantity and quality of sleep directly affect your mental and physical health and in consequence, the quality of your life.

Lack of restorative sleep reduces the body's ability to fight infections and also compromises the cardiovascular abilities.

It affects your creativity, productivity, emotional balance, the immune system, and your brain and heart's functioning. The list goes on.

To be honest, no other activity has the potential to provide so many benefits with so little effort.

A lot of achievers feel that sleeping means shutting down your body and moving away from your dreams.

It's certainly not so.

A ton of research says that our brain is super busy performing and overseeing the necessary biological maintenance while we sleep. Sleep keeps our body in top working condition and turbocharges us by preparing us for the day ahead.

If we deprive ourselves of the required hours of deep restorative sleep, we simultaneously deny ourselves the ability to perform, create and communicate at the level of our true potential. Without sleep, we are on the path of mental, emotional and physical break-down.

Myth Alert: Most of us feel that getting one hour less sleep isn't a big deal.

That's certainly not true. It may happen that you do not feel sleepy throughout the day. Still, it may reduce your ability to think clearly and respond quickly.

Let's get tactical now.

Usually, one sleep cycle consists of 1.5 hours or 90 minutes. It may be a little different for you, though that's the universal standard.

For an adult to function in Beast-mode, one must aim for at least 6 hours (4 sleep cycles) to 7.5 hours (5 sleep cycles).

Please do remember to add another 15 to 30 minutes as you take some time to go off to sleep.

The Ultimate Advantage Pro-Tip:

Power Nap – Weapon of Mass Restoration

If your day allows you the luxury to take a short nap, go for it!

Sleep studies have found a lot of evidence that brief periods of naps are critical to renew and sustain peak energy over long hours.

Some of the legends who were fans of napping are Albert Einstein, Thomas Edison, Winston Churchill, Bill Clinton, and Napoleon Bonaparte, to name a few.

If that isn't proof enough, then please read NASA's findings given below.

NASA's Fatigue Counter Measures Program found that a short nap substantially improved performance by an average of 34 per cent and alertness by 100 per cent.

Also, in a study conducted by Harvard researchers, it was found that subjects whose performance dropped by as much as 50 per cent in a day were able to completely restore their highest levels of performance after a one-hour nap in the early afternoon.

Sleep Doctor Michael Breus recommends us to aim for a power nap after 8 hours of waking up. He also suggests NOT to nap after 3:30 P.M. as it may disrupt your ability to fall asleep that night, especially if you're early to bed.

The ideal recommended time for a power nap (keeping in mind the different stages of the sleep cycle) is 20 minutes.

However, if you still do not feel your best after a 20-minute nap, then go up to one hour, or an hour and a half.

Dr Breus recommends us to set aside 30 minutes for a power nap, as it should take you 10 minutes to fall asleep (if you fall asleep faster than 10 minutes then you are likely sleep-deprived and you really need to work on your sleep patterns!). Do use an alarm clock to keep track of time.

"Don't think you will be doing less work because you sleep during the day. That's a foolish notion held by people who have no imagination. You will accomplish more. You get two days in one—well, at least one and a half, I'm sure."

*—**Winston Churchill***

2. Peak - Ease - Repeat

Over time, science has discovered the importance of biological rhythm in our lives. This particular field of study, also known as *chronobiology*, examines and emphasises the relationship between our natural rhythms with respect to time.

How does 'chronobiology' matter to us?

This may seem like a mere piece of science trivia, but if we can understand how these internal rhythms operate, we can use it to maximise our peak energy to perform at virtuoso level throughout the day.

In the 1950s, sleep researcher Nathaniel Kleitman discovered that the human body tends to operate in rhythm, i.e. cycles of 90-120 minutes. During the night, these cycles relate to the different stages of sleep. During the day, these cycles relate to varying levels of energy and alertness.

Nathaniel Klietman named this phenomenon as the "Basic Rest Activity Cycle" (BRAC).

Nathaniel Klietman elaborated that we can perform at our peak levels for about 90 minutes as per our biological rhythm. But after 90 minutes or so, our body reaches its saturation point and performance starts to decline. It starts craving for rest and recovery.

In essence, every 90-120 minutes, our body experiences a period of massive energy and alertness followed by exhaustion.

During the cycle of massive bursts of energy, we can get a lot done. However, the problem arises if we continue to work and ignore the body's need for rest.

We may end up on the losing side of the battle, where we may try hard to play full out, but end up accomplishing nothing much at all only because we were running on empty.

PEAK EASE REPEAT
(Infinite Loop of Peak Performance)

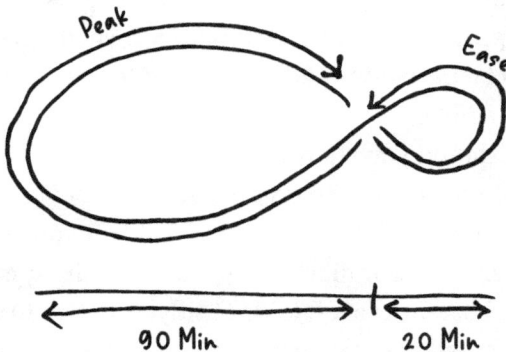

Peak   Ease

90 Min   20 Min

Think about it. Isn't this the pattern in which all the greatest business people and creative producers work?

Short intervals of intense extraordinary focus and energy, and they pull back to recover in between each interval.

That is precisely what I call the 'Peak-Ease-Repeat' loop.

The Peak-Ease-Repeat loop refers to the cycle where you go all-in for the first 90 minutes of your high performing energy cycle. Then you pull back and recover, replenish and refuel yourself before embarking on the next cycle of productivity.

You keep on repeating this cycle throughout the day, to not only put in the hours but also bring enormous value to the hours you put in.

In short, rather than being in an endless 'marathon', we must consciously choose to be in a series of powerful, bursting with energy, and eager-to-push 'sprints'!

Now the vital question is, how do you optimise your healing during the 20-minute break?

Social media, is it?

Not at all. Though social media may help you relax, it's a highly addictive trance and can suck your valuable time. You might end up scrolling for hours and hours before you come back to your senses.

You may consider social media as a mental and emotional equivalent of eating junk food. Similar to junk food, social media may provide you with a temporary form of recovery, but it will rarely be nutritious and more often than not, it is easy to consume too much.

So, what should you choose to do?

What you may choose to do instead, is to move and stretch by going for a walk, listen to music, focus on your breathing, drink some green tea or maybe chat with a 'positive' co-worker.

The Peak-Ease-Repeat cycle is not only restricted to your days. To sustain consistent peak performance and energy, you may extrapolate the same phenomenon in your weeks and months.

After going all-in and working intensely for five days a week, take at least a day or two off to recover and replenish yourself.

You may choose to go off the radar by shunning technology, spending quality time with family, reading a book, watching your favourite movies etc.

3. Nutrition

Can you imagine what a World Class Olympic Champion's diet would be like, especially when preparing for a big game?

I am sure you cannot, even in your wildest dream, imagine him to have a pitcher of beer with fish and chips!

Why can you not imagine that?

It is because you acknowledge the fact that having such a meal will diminish his performance for the big game.

You are aware that he has to have a stringent diet which en-sures that he receives all the proper nutrition. Proper nutrition primes him with world-class peak energy required to unleash the outstanding genius that resides within him.

How about you?

What's your diet like?

Does it qualify you to compete in the race to realise your Epic Life Vision?

We all understand that proper nutrition is vital and is the absolute core of our energy level. We must embrace a sustain-able and healthy diet that includes low-toxicity foods and es-sential nutrients and oils required by our body to perform at extraordinary levels.

The food you eat today defines your energy and also your health in the long run. It affects your moods and determines your longevity.

Yet most of the people I know, fail in this category. Why?

There are primarily 3 reasons for this:

1. They do not know.
2. They do not care.
3. They know, they care, but they cannot help it – These are the ones who 'live to eat' and not 'eat to live'?

What if you belong to the category who 'live to eat' and cer-tainly not 'eat to live'? Are you doomed?

Before I answer that, I must share something with you.

I am sure that you are committed to a life of excellence, or you wouldn't have reached this part of the book.

Thus, I encourage you to consider yourself a champion athlete and take your diet to the next level by putting in the proper nutrition required to win the game.

I urge you to eat to win by recalibrating your diet. Try to incorporate as many fruits and vegetables and get rid of processed food.

If you're serious about becoming a champion, start eating like one.

But don't worry, if that's something you cannot do or resist, all is not lost. You can still make up (not all, but some of it) by having a cheat day, controlling the timing of your intake of food and last but certainly not least, by exercising and working out.

4. Hydrate

Now you may ask "How is water related to energy and performance?'.

Surprisingly, most headaches and fatigue in life are caused not by stress, not by eye strain but because of dehydration!

Now, what comes next may seem like common sense, but it's not a common practice. On that account, even at the risk of sounding cliché, I must pen it. This is Biology 101.

Water is an essential and significant component of all living matter, including human beings. The human body needs water to survive. It is vital for all critical processes including digestion, blood circulation and excretion. Every organ and cell needs to stay hydrated for the body to function at its optimum level.

For our understanding of energy, we find tons of research which elucidate that staying hydrated optimises the brain, elevates your mood and scales-up your energy.

Ideally, 2-3 litres of water is sufficient to keep ourselves hydrated for peak performance, but how would you know what's adequate for you?

An excellent way to determine what's sufficient and what's not is to check the colour of your urine. If the colour is dark, you need to drink more water. If your urine is light or has no colour, then you are well hydrated.

Some people struggle to drink water because they don't like the taste. Drinking something that tastes like nothing can get boring. There are ways to improve water taste by adding fruits and herbs such as lemon, cucumber or mint. Try spicing it up to stay hydrated.

5. Move

Humans are designed to move!

What do I mean by that?

The body that we enjoy today results from evolution through movement and being one with nature.

It results from being on the move (to hunt or to avoid being hunted by the sabre-toothed tiger). It results from walking, climbing, jumping, crawling and swimming, farming and dancing around the fire. These are all the movements the body is designed for.

But today, we live in a society where nobody moves anymore.

If you visit an orthopaedist, he would confirm that people don't see him because they got injured while cycling or playing football. They usually come up to him because they hurt their back while bending down to pick up the pencil they dropped on the floor!

Injured one's back by bending down to pick up the pencil? Really?

Yes, it's because we don't move anymore. Our cars are shiny, but our bodies are rusted.

Our body is made up of individual parts which combine to operate as a unified identity. To function in an optimised way, every aspect must perform with ease and efficiency to generate peak power.

You cannot execute your lofty ambitions when your back hurts or when your shoulder is aching to move.

You get the idea, right? We need to move to ensure our incredible body is in a power state to perform consistently over the long term.

So, how does one move?

You may choose to move by either stretching, doing strength training or cardiovascular exercises. Along with that, if you want to be a heavyweight champion in terms of peak energy, you may choose to mix it all up and do it all in a planned manner.

Taking out time to exercise and lift weights for at least 30 minutes a day has been proven to benefit all bodily systems. It also helps in the protection of muscle mass as you age. Exercising will make you look better, feel stronger and fill you up with a plethora of vibrant energy.

If weight-lifting isn't your thing, you may choose to go out and brisk-walk or jog, swim or do Zumba. Or you may decide to do yoga, play your favourite OUTDOOR sport, cycle, row, or do planks, push-ups and burpees or whatever works for you.

Please take note; **Exercise is optional, MOVEMENT is Essential.**

Remember: if you are just starting, you will feel tired and exhausted the first few weeks rather than energised. It is natural as your body is now adjusting to your new way of living. It's not real fatigue; it's only transitional fatigue.

A sweet reminder is not to think of movement as a fun activity. Though if you have fun while doing it, there's nothing like it. You have to do it even if you don't have fun. Be in this for extraordinary energy.

When you move, your body releases certain chemicals called 'endorphins' that leave you feeling renewed and fulfilled like never before. This does wonder to your energy levels.

Not only that. When you move and sweat, your body releases a chemical called BDNF (Brain-derived Neurotrophic Factor). BDNF helps in repairs of brain cells that are impaired by stress. It also expedites the way your brain processes and executes information.

Please consult an expert about developing an effective movement plan that is best suited for you and your body.

6. Breathe

What is the single most crucial rhythm that is required to keep you alive?

It's pretty obvious once you think about it.

You need to be able to 'breathe' to be alive.

Surprisingly, we breathe on auto-mode, and most of us never think about breathing. Still, the pivotal question is, 'Are you breathing right?'

To this, you might think, "If I am alive, I must be breathing right!"

Are you ready to burst your bubble? If yes, then the first thing you must do is compare your breathing to that of a new-born baby.

You would notice that a new-born breathes via their belly, i.e., when they inhale their belly expands and when they exhale, their belly contracts. This is indeed the perfect form of breathing, also known as **Diaphragmatic** breathing.

On the contrary, most likely, you would be breathing shallow via your chest, and you would notice that your belly doesn't move at all.

Remarkably, stress causes shallow breathing, and shallow breathing causes further stress. As a result, when our breathing is shallow, our body is stuck in a downward spiral of anxiety and stress.

John Luckovich, an integrative breathwork facilitator in Brooklyn, New York states, "Shallow breathing doesn't just make stress a response, it makes stress a habit for our bodies, and therefore, our minds are locked into".

In the long term, if we continue to breathe in a shallow way, it can seriously affect our health.

On the other hand, diaphragmatic breathing can help lower blood pressure, reduce heart rate, relax muscles, decrease stress. It can massively increase our energy levels.

So, how do we breathe from our diaphragm?

Complicated as it sounds, it's quite simple.

All you need to do is correct your posture to not slouch and make sure that your chest is wide. If you do this one simple correction, you will notice your belly go in and out like that of a new-born baby.

Deep, smooth and rhythmic breathing is simultaneously a source of energy, alertness and focus, as well as of relaxation, stillness and quiet—the ultimate healthy pulse.

The Ultimate Advantage Pro-Tip:

Instant Magic of Power Breathing: Inhale to a count of 3 seconds, hold for 12 seconds and exhale for 6 seconds. (Ratio of 1:4:2)

Extending the exhalation prompts a powerful wave of recovery.

This exercise of power breaths lowers arousal and quiets not just the body but also the mind and the emotions.

7. Proximity with Turbo-Chargers

The way you feel is the way you ultimately perform.

Who, apart from you, do you think has the most significant impact over how you feel?

People you surround yourself with.

Think about it.

Have you ever spent time with someone whose energy and enthusiasm was so powerful and contagious that it somehow inspired you?

On the contrary, how different was it when compared to spending time with a person who always complains, from the amount of salt in the food to the weather to absolutely everything?

I am almost sure that spending time with the latter got you feeling agitated and sucked energy away from the moment.

This phenomenon is often referred to as "Emotional Contagion". What it means is that you can catch and adopt the emotions, attitudes, behaviour and results from people you spend time with. Sooner or later, you start to think the way they think and behave the way they behave.

It happens without any conscious effort, just like you could catch a cold or the flu from others.

Simply put, who you are around and what they think, say, do and become also has the power to impact and set the course of your life.

> You are the average of the five people you spend the most time with."
>
> **—Jim Rohn**

Experts say that your peer group is the biggest indicator and predictor of success and failure in your life. So, if you take a close look at your peer group and analyse their path, you can quickly determine what your future would look like.

❝ *The people you habitually associate with determine as much as 95 per cent of your success or failure in life.*"
—Dr David McClelland of Harvard University

Why am I telling you this?

Simply for you to acknowledge and take charge.

There are two kinds of people in your life – The Energy Drainers and The Turbo-Chargers.

The first kind will infect you and make you settle for mediocrity, as that's the level they are themselves playing at. They tend to hold you back, to steal your joy and to diminish your fire. They are the Nay-Sayers who always see how bad the world is.

The turbo-chargers are the ones who lift you. They boost you up and inspire you to be your greatest self. They hold you up for a higher standard and propel you to keep going forward no matter what!

You will have both kinds of people in your life, but you cannot hang out with the energy drainers and hope to achieve your Epic Life Vision.

They are the ones who will laugh at you, mock you and make fun of you for even trying.

So, what do you do now?

What I suggest with the utmost care and love for you is to consciously architect your social environment. You must either commit to removing the Energy Drainers from your life altogether or if that's not possible, try to spend as little time with them. It may not be easy at first, but remember, the life you deserve depends on it!

On the other hand, when it comes to the Turbo-Chargers, spend most of your time with them– brainstorm and mastermind with them and make them your accountability partners.

You must protect your association with turbo-chargers and try to create a community where you have more of them into your life. If you do, you shall see your life take a whole new route altogether.

> **The Ultimate Advantage Pro-Tip:**
>
> *Who is the one person you spend the most time with?*
>
> *It's a no-brainer. The one person you spend not only the most but all of your time with is no one but YOU!*
>
> *Surprisingly, you have the gift to turbocharge yourself, and you may not know it yet.*
>
> *Now you may be wondering, "How can I do that?".*
>
> *By consciously deciding to use words that fuel and elevate you.*
>
> *For instance, if I had to tell myself "I need to write my book today", I could simply change the words and turbocharge myself in an instant.*
>
> *For instance, I can tell myself, "I will make massive progress in writing my book today so that I can become a BEST-SELLING AUTHOR and I can IMPACT and INFLUENCE MILLIONS of people and help them to transform their lives!"*
>
> *The number of words has increased, but can you feel the emotional jolt I would go through if I used the second sentence instead of the first?*
>
> *Remember, you can turbocharge yourself in an instant.*

8. Emotional Nourishment

66 *No one ever said on their deathbed, 'I wish I'd spent more time in the office.'"*

— Rabbi Harold Kushner

Ponder for a minute about your own life -

How much time do you spend at work and how much time do you spend on activities that provide you with a deep sense of joy and satisfaction?

Fun and enjoyment are a great source of recovery and emotional nourishment. Doing things that make you happy, inevitably prompts a positive emotional charge and generates more energy.

Depending on your interests, you may choose to have fun while engaging in singing, dancing, theatre, reading a book, playing a sport, visiting a museum, attending a concert, hanging out with friends or going for a vacation with your family.

Also, fun and enjoyment don't always have to be flamboyant.

Sometimes, people derive fun and enjoyment by merely spending time alone in solitude and reflecting. That's when they enter the zone of genius: **the zone of transient hypofrontality.**

(Transient what..!? We shall cover this magnificent concept in detail in the bonus chapter - 'Thank God It's Morning'. Don't you miss out on this!)

All the virtuosos and heavyweight champions of the industry got their best ideas and their most creative insights when they were relaxed and were having fun. Scientists call it the incubation period of your thoughts and ideas, i.e., a period when your best ideas are incubating while you are relaxing and having fun.

To sum it all up, Emotional Nourishment in terms of fun and enjoyment is a critical ingredient for being in the Power State.

9. Meditation and gratitude

What do you tend to focus on?

Do you tend to focus on the things that you have or the things that you don't?

If you are like most people, then I am sure you too end up focusing on the things you don't have. That leads to anxiety, stress, frustration and a lot of mental issues.

Mental health is critical. If you can develop a ritual to meditate, you can fortify your mind and soul in the most positive and life-altering way. It's a form of prayer one must do every day for a fulfilling life.

Meditation is like jet fuel to your mind and soul. It provides you with mental clarity, and you feel more connected to yourself and the world.

Do you know that your mind is like a parachute? Yes, it is. Similar to a parachute, it only works when it's open. And meditation helps you open your mind.

Also, no matter where you are in life, you will always want to grow and achieve more. There will always be numerous things you want but don't have.

However, if you DO NOT appreciate what you already have, you will always live a life of lack, no matter how much you have or achieve.

Hence, only an attitude of gratitude can help you with peace of mind and live a more prosperous life with greater positivity.

> 66 *I cried because I had no shoes,*
> *then I met a man who had no feet."*
>
> — *Anonymous*

The Ultimate Advantage Pro-Tip:

Do not JUST make a list of things you are grateful for. Feel the positive emotions associated with it.

Follow up on these 9 rituals of the 'Pyramid of Vitality', and you will be able to enter the Power State of peak energy. It shall empower you with the X-Factor of High performers and enable you to perform and operate at peak levels for an extended period of time.

The outcome of this chapter was to realise that you may be the smartest person in the room. You may have a billion-dollar idea with the talent and skills to achieve it. You may also have a future filled with pure opportunities. But without a Power State of world-class physical, mental, and emotional energy, you'll never be able to produce world-class results.

You just won't.

Ask yourself, would you want to reach the end of your life and find out that you lived just $1/10^{th}$ of it? Not because you didn't care, but because you were too tired and didn't have the energy to go for it.

Be warned: At the end, you don't want to end up saying,

I could have.....
I would have.....
I should have.....

As I keep saying, there's always a choice.
Choose wisely!

The next chapter is a bonus chapter that combines and brings about the best of Productivity and Power State of Peak Energy. It's about a strategy that helps you kickstart your day and transform your life from "Oh God it's Morning" to...

SIX

THANK GOD IT'S MORNING
The Ultimate Morning Advantage

W hat's the one sure-shot secret to having an Epic Life?

It's simple. If you keep having Epic days constantly and consistently, you will end up having an Epic Life.

Makes sense?

Now, while reading this book, you may be all pumped up about achieving your Epic Life Vision.

But, do you think you will be able to get up every morning as excited and passionate as you are now? Do you think you will jump up every day, raring to go and make your dream a reality?

Let's admit it; it won't always happen that way.

The hardest thing in the world is to get up and give your 100% each day and keep going at it no matter what.

That's the real grind!

No matter how disciplined, dedicated, determined, and desperate you are, there will be days when you would wake up and say to yourself, "Oh God, it's morning. I do not want another day of hustle".

On these days, you wouldn't care about your Epic Life Vision. That's called life.

But, you also cannot expect to achieve your dream if you do not hustle and get going even on days when you're not excited and passionate.

So the critical question is, how can one generate excitement and passion even on days when they're not?

The secret lies in hacking your morning. It would be best if you primed your morning to empower and optimise your day to make massive progress towards your dream.

How does one do that?

To find out the answer, let us embark on a journey from 'Oh God, it's morning', to 'THANK GOD it's morning.'

This is a suggested framework where you start your day by **'THANK GOD'**!

What do I mean by that?

THANK GOD is a Framework wherein we incorporate the key habits and rituals of super achievers that help us kick-start and prime our day.

So here it goes,

T| Transient Hypofrontality (As promised earlier)

H| Hydrate yourself

A| Amplify your mind

N| Ninja Workout

K| Kind Reflection

G | Gratitude

O | Organise your day

D | Daily Mission Mastery

T| Transient Hypofrontality:
The Zone of Ultimate Genius
and Epic Performance.

This is one of the most incredible skills you possess, and yet you may know nothing about it!

Would you want to know what it is?

Have you heard about Bill Gates's 'Think Week'?

If you haven't, then let me help you take a closer look.

Every year the iconic billionaire Bill Gates goes off and spends a week in his holiday home. He spends the week in complete solitude (without any distractions including but not limited to Social Media, News, and Emails) and thinks monomaniacally about possibilities on how to change and impact the world.

The Think Week has helped Bill Gates get away from the 'fixed and normal thinking' of the world into the valley of creativity. It enabled him to gain uncommon but meaningful and enriching insights. It helped him enter the "FLOW" state of ultimate genius and epic performance.

Would you want to understand and apply it so that you too could be a heavy-weight champion at whatever you do?

Now you would say, "Koonal I do not have the luxury of time or money like Bill Gates to go for a Think Week!"

But hang on for a moment.

Before rejecting the idea, kindly be aware that all great producers and epic performers from Steve Jobs to Thomas Edison, Picasso to Mozart, Elon Musk to Mark Zuckerberg, Ratan Tata to Dhirubhai Ambani, spent/spend a lot of their time in solitude. Solitude helped them unleash their ultimate advantage.

What if I tell you, you could do it every day within the confines of your home, and it costs nothing. Yes, you read it right. That is possible!

Dr Arne Dietrich, a professor and brain researcher, calls this phenomenon 'Transient Hypofrontality'. If you can understand and apply it, you too can unleash your A-game.

Please do take some time to understand this. It may take some effort to understand and absorb, but it's worth it!

The word Transient means 'temporary', Hypo means 'slow', and frontality means 'the prefrontal cortex of the brain'. In essence, transient hypofrontality is nothing but a fancy word for 'temporary slowing down of the brain's prefrontal cortex.

Now you may be wondering, what is the prefrontal cortex of the brain?

Stay with me, please.

The prefrontal cortex is the CEO or the logical part of the brain. Whenever you are engaged in deep thinking and problem solving, this section of the brain is hyperactive, and it helps you sail through.

Not only that, but the prefrontal cortex also controls the inner dialogue, the self-critic, the mental chatter and the constant worrying.

Have you ever had a great idea, but something inside of you said, "it's not possible" or "you cannot do it". It then led to you doubting the feasibility of the idea, and therefore you never acted upon it.

If you have, then please be aware that all the logic and reasoning of why you couldn't do it, was provided by your inner critic –the prefrontal cortex.

Why am I explaining complicated science jargons to you?

Here's the real deal: If you can temporarily silence your inner critic, you too can enter the zone of FLOW where outstanding performance begins. Maybe you too can change the world like Gates and Jobs!

This is where your true genius shows up, and time seems to slow down. Your creativity begins to explode, and you can now see solutions that were hazy and blurred before.

Sounds impressive, right?

Knowing what Transient Hypofrontality is good and all, but how do you induce it in your daily life?

To induce transient hypofrontality, all you need to do is build a wall that fortifies and guards your focus and attention. This can be done every morning when you get up as your brain is in alpha state, which helps you to quickly drop into transient frontality.

It's sad to know, but most of us get up in the morning frantically searching for our cell phones. We crave to satiate our hunger for social media, email, news or our preferred mode of distraction.

What we need to do is create an environment that is devoid of any distractions and interruptions (where electronic devices are switched off and no one can disturb us). We need to obsessively focus and immerse ourselves on the needle-movers, i.e., the most important opportunities we have on hand.

Simply put, you need to turn off the notifications on your phone and turn on the notifications of your desires, hopes and aspirations.

You may think I am crazy and this is all rah-rah!

But think about it, when do you get your best and life-changing ideas? Do you get them when you're in solitude or when you are rushing to work and busy running in and out of meetings?

This, I believe, is the single most powerful weapon to help you journey from where you are to where you want to be. And this tool is available to you daily.

You may practice the ritual of Transient Hypofrontality right after you get up by going out for a walk and enjoying nature or by sitting alone and thinking in a quiet room, whatever works for you.

The Ultimate Advantage Pro-Tip:

Wake up between 4 A.M. and 6 A.M. every day so that there are no distractions, interruptions and over-simulations as most people you know would be sleeping at this time. While the world is busy sleeping, you are in the beautiful process of designing your life.

No wonder, most great men and women throughout history, rose early and lived with purpose.

But the pressing question is, will you create the necessary conditions to experience it?

If you do and do it consistently, your life will never be the same.

H| Hydrate Yourself

As discussed in the Pyramid of Vitality, hydration is crucial. Though it is great to have water all day long, starting your day with a glass of water helps you kick start your day in the right direction.

From times immemorial, we have been told to start our day by drinking water. It may seem so effortless and straightforward, but somehow, most people miss doing it.

Even at the cost of blabbering and repeating a cliché, I would like to elucidate the importance of having water first thing in the morning so that you never miss it.

- Helps fight Dehydration: When you get up, your body has had a 6-8 hour of water fasting. It's dehydrated. Water enables you to get hydrated quickly. It also helps with your lower bowel movement.

- Helps you get alert and provides a burst of energy: The biggest cause of lethargy and low energy is that you are dehydrated. Having water first thing in the morning can help your body get work-ready as it boosts your energy and alertness.

- Helps in Removing toxins: When you sleep, your body repairs itself and casts out all the toxins in the body. When you drink water on an empty stomach in the morning, your body flushes out these harmful toxins, leaving a fresh and healthy body.

A | Amplify your mind and soul

66 *Your real self may be hiding somewhere, look for it within, when you find yourself, you can freely be what you want to be."*

— ***Michael Bassey Johnson***

High performers do not start their day until they meditate. This is the secret sauce. Do you wonder why?

As a high performer, you will have to encounter stress. Stress is where achievement and desires meet, and meditation helps you release stress.

In short, meditation is like jet fuel to your mind and soul.

It helps you amplify your mind and soul as it provides you with mental clarity, and you end up feeling more connected to yourself and the world. Clarity always precedes mastery, and this practice will deepen your focus throughout the day.

You may also choose to turbo-charge and amplify your mind-set by feeding it with positivity. You may read a book, listen to a podcast or watch videos that inspire you to stretch your limits and be the best version of yourself.

N| Ninja-Workout

As discussed in the Pyramid of Vitality, movement is vital for optimum health. If you can start your day with it, there is nothing like it.

To take it a notch higher, if you can move or workout like a Ninja and get your blood pumping, you are sure to be on fire the rest of the day.

A ton of research proves working out in the morning helps you feel happier and more optimistic throughout the day. Moreover, working out like a ninja and sweating will reward you with a release of Dopamine (helps in motivation), endorphins, serotonin and BDNF. These feel-good chemicals help elevate your mood and eradicate stress.

Please don't get me wrong; I am not suggesting you workout for an hour. What I am suggesting is that even if you work out for 10 minutes, do it like a Ninja, and your work is done.

Ninja workout also helps to amp up your transient hypofrontality quotient.

Take a moment to ponder: if you work out like a Ninja by being engaged in an intense physical exercise, where your heart is beating out of your chest, and your muscles are on fire, is there room for thinking about anything else let alone your problems in life?

Makes sense?

I hope it does.

Thus, we can safely conclude that ninja workout is a great way to start the day. Moreover, if you workout like a ninja you are guaranteed to feel happier: as now you know that you have activated your day by doing something that helps you move towards your Epic Life Vision of a healthy you.

Let us now move on to the next aspect.

K| Kind reflection

66 Life can only be understood backwards,
but it must be lived forwards."
— Søren Kierkegaard

Reflection helps us to look, think about and connect with our past. It helps us to take and absorb key learnings. It also enriches our lives by providing us with priceless insights that will guide our present and future.

Let's not forget that all super-achievers have failed many times. They never ruminate and complain; instead, they reflect by being kind to themselves and learn from their mistakes. It's one of the hidden secrets. They reflected, learned from their failures and changed their approach until they finally made it.

Now, what do you do if your past haunts you and you do not want to revisit it?

Hey listen: all the suffering, all the negativity, all the wounds of your past can ignite a fire within you. You decide whether you let the fire kill you or be the burning desire and motivation for you to be world-class.

Also, I'm only requesting you to ask yourself empowering questions. On that account, the past will help you move forward and prevent you from repeating the same mistakes in future. Hence, kind reflection makes mistakes a valuable learning tool, instead of feeling embarrassed or upset about.

Reflect upon your learnings from life so that you don't repeat them.

Do not get stuck in your past. Rather ask yourself –

- What can I learn from my past?
- What will I no longer settle for?
- What excuses will I release?
- How do I want to be remembered?

The first few times you reflect, you might get generic and obvious answers. But as you keep going more in-depth, you will uncover gold in the form of invaluable wisdom nuggets.

Kind Reflection can recode and rewire you and prime you for success.

Remember to be kind and not beat yourself up while reflecting.

G| Gratitude

By practicing gratitude, you enable yourself to see the good side of life. (As discussed in the Pyramid of Vitality – Chapter 5.)

No matter where you are in life, there's no better way to start your day than by thinking about at least 3 things you are grateful for. That's how you prime yourself with positivity to tackle your day.

But what do you do if you're having to go through a terrible phase in life and can't think of anything to be grateful for?

If you can't think of anything, be grateful for the air you breathe, be thankful for being able to think.

Be creative and look around. I'm sure you will surprise yourself with the things you took for granted.

O| Organise your day

What's the best way to run your day and not let your day run you?

Organise your day by first reviewing your goals and capturing all the ideas, thoughts, follow-ups etc.

You may then plan and schedule your day based on prioritised outcomes, i.e., results you need to accomplish today.

Kindly remember NOT to be seduced by the to-do list (as discussed in chapter 4).

Let's not forget; productivity is about moving towards your goals and dreams and not just about getting things done!

You do not want to end your day where you were busy ticking off from your to-do list only to realise you didn't progress at all. We don't want to be running on a treadmill called life.

You may also want to check your weekly schedule and identify outcomes/tasks you had committed for this day.

> **The Ultimate Advantage Pro-Tip:**
>
> While planning your day, schedule things that require brain work, planning and strategising for the first half of the day. You may schedule Operational and routine work for the second half of the day.

D| Daily Mission Mastery (DM²)

Once you have organised your day, ask yourself:

What is my mission for today? What must I accomplish today to progress my life? What specific results do I have to create today that will help make the 90-day goal or a 1-year target a reality? What outcome will I achieve today, no matter what?

This is what I call Daily Mission Mastery or DM².

This helps you gain massive momentum in designing and creating the life you desire. If you follow DM² religiously, you would have achieved a minimum of 365 outcomes towards your epic life vision at the end of the year.

Good news: The more you achieve, the more energy you get to achieve. Psychologically, every time you achieve or complete something, you build momentum. If you can get completion energy every day, you become unstoppable.

Author James Clear illustrated this beautifully in his book "Atomic Habits". He said, small daily wins compounded over time and when done consistently lead to stunning and unbelievable results.

$$\left(1.00\right)^{365} = 1.00$$

$$\left(1.01\right)^{365} = 37.7$$

Doing nothing at all
Vs
1% Better Everyday

Please never-ever doubt this: A great life is never built overnight. It always seems so, but it's always built one day at a time.

And having a deliberate and purposeful morning routine can lay the rock-solid foundation for success.

All in all, the 'T.H.A.N.K G.O.D.' framework helps you start the day with power and purpose. It provides you with the required momentum to make the Epic Life Vision a reality. That's what I call **M.S.M.E.**

Now you might say, "Koonal, what is M.S.M.E !??".

M.S.M.E. means Momentum Sticks while Motivation Evaporates. *M.S.M.E is the real deal. Please be warned: to make your dream a reality what you need is Momentum and NOT Motivation. As sooner or later, motivation will evaporate and fizzle out!*

If you want to make sure that your momentum sticks, do not stop; continue to the next chapter. The next chapter is crucial as it guides you to a skill that helps fast track your way towards your vision. It opens up various new avenues for making your EPIC LIFE VISION a reality. Let's discover...

SEVEN

PEOPLE FACTOR
The Strategic Art Of Mastering Influence

" Leadership is influence, nothing more and nothing less."

— John C Maxwell

In 1908, there was an Artist in Vienna, Austria. He was slightly under-average in height, had a receding hairline with thin lips. And he was someone who was often known to offer weak handshakes with moist clammy hands.

He lived by himself, like a nomad, moving from one place to another. Soon his savings started to dwindle, and his lifestyle spiralled downwards.

Eventually, after all his savings were exhausted, he ended up sleeping on park benches and started begging for money. As you would have visualised, he was a dirty, smelly, unshaven man wearing tattered clothes. He was broke to the extent that he didn't even have the money to buy an overcoat to withstand the freezing winter of Europe.

In December 1909, freezing and half-starved, he somehow managed to survive by moving into a shelter for the homeless and eating at a soup kitchen operated by nuns from a nearby convent.

This man was an artist who could barely make ends meet.

Just for fun, let's contrast this man with another artist - one of the most influential and notorious dictators of the 20th century, the leader of Germany's Nazi party – Adolf Hitler.

Adolf Hitler was an artist who liked to live life grandly. Though he was a political leader, he generated enormous wealth through writing and copyright fees by selling his photographs. He was an art connoisseur and had a comprehensive collection of rare and exotic art pieces worldwide.

Hitler, also known as the Führer (meaning the absolute authority), single-handedly built the architecture of the 2nd World War. He had successfully conquered a dozen nations and mercilessly slaughtered as many as 21 million people.

He is often disregarded for the state-sponsored mass murder of over 6 million Jews, which he did for no reason other than his dislike for them.

Aren't the two descriptions above fascinatingly contrasting – An artist who couldn't make ends meet and another who made the world come to its knees.

What if I told you that the above two stories were of the same man!

Yes, that's correct. The homeless artist was none other than Adolf Hitler.

But the vital question is, how did the homeless artist rise to become a tyrant?

The answer is quite fascinating.

Hitler was able to transform his life by mastering the art of impacting and influencing others to gain control.

But wait a minute, is that the objective of me writing this chapter: to enable and transform you to become a dictator like Hitler?

Absolutely not!

Although, I would definitely urge you to think about something.

Why is it that leaders like Adolf Hitler, Mahatma Gandhi, Mother Teresa, Donald Trump, Barack Obama, Oprah Winfrey, Martin Luther King, Nelson Mandela could communicate in a way where they could impact and influence millions of people, whereas an average salesperson can't even impact and influence a homemaker to buy the best quality television in the market?

Hey listen, it doesn't matter whether you like the leaders mentioned above or not. It doesn't even matter if you agree or disagree with what they stood for. But what truly matters for us to succeed, is to understand how these legendary leaders were able to create a culture of loyal and raving fans who always stood by them, no matter what.

Aren't you curious, was there something special in the way these great influencers said and did things?

Was there a strategy behind the madness they could create?

The answer is 'yes'!

All leaders had mastered the strategic art of influence to connect with people in a way that made others believe in them, listen to them, follow them and buy from them. They were able to influence others to take actions that they recommended.

Before we proceed, it would be prudent to define what influence means.

Influence is the power to affect the character/behaviour of someone or something, to make them believe and/or make them commit to taking the recommended action.

Thomas J. Stanley, a celebrated author who obsessively researched and studied the self-made affluent American millionaires, found that the common denominator for driving success was their ability to deal with and influence others.

Take a moment to ponder.

How good would a lawyer be if he weren't able to communicate effectively and convince the jury that his client is innocent? He may be the smartest and most intelligent lawyer with a degree from the best Law School on the face of the planet. But would it mean anything at all if he had no impact and influence on the jury's decision?

The same logic applies to all walks of life.

Are you aware of the fact that Jack Ma, (the founder of the multi-billion-dollar company Alibaba.com), was able to convince a group of investors to invest $2,00,00,000 in his company based on a single piece of hand-written paper?

No project report and no business plan. Just a sheet of paper. Really!

Then why is it that other start-ups (with equally good business ideas that have the potential to change the world), prepare heaps of optimistic projections and reports but fail to encash the opportunity when they meet investors?

It's simply because of the way they communicate.

While Jack Ma could communicate in a way that impacted and influenced the investors' emotions to believe in him and invest in his vision, the others might have failed to impact the investors' emotions. Maybe, they kept focusing only on the projections and numbers.

A friend of mine, Rajiv, is a courteous gentleman. He possesses all the qualities of being the perfect groom. However, as I am writing this book, he is still single, and he has never been able to date anyone. Can you guess why?

He wasn't able to communicate effectively and influence a girl to go on a date with him.

If you look around, you too will notice that some people with less talent and less knowledge get jobs over skilled and talented people. They get the job only because they were more likeable.

You will find a man with no job, no money and perhaps even a history of being a cheater, getting the girl over the guy who had it all. It is simply because he could use his charm to influence her.

It sounds unfair, but it's the bitter reality of life.

But what if you already have all the money you need and you are not interested in anything I just mentioned.

Do you still need to master impact and influence?

Let's find out.

Why do you think criminals are sentenced to solitary confinement for committing a heinous crime? Why are they not allowed to interact with others?

They are given solitary confinement because the legal system is aware of how solitary confinement (an environment devoid of any human interaction) eats up the human soul.

As social animals, we crave interaction and relationships with the people around us.

Relationships empower and nourish the soul. More often than not, if we do not have enough healthy interactions with other beings, a stable mind becomes unstable. Relationships are the essential ingredient that defines the quality of our lives emotionally, spiritually, physically, mentally and financially.

For that reason alone, you must master your ability to communicate and influence.

Influence is the foundational key that differentiates people who are successful and fulfilled from those who almost always fail and end up lonely and depressed.

The ability to communicate and influence effectively gives you the ultimate advantage of transferring necessary information and connecting with others by developing trust. It also helps by increasing understanding amongst each other, which would, in turn, help to resolve conflicts amicably.

Isn't this what ultimately leads to a strong and healthy relationship?

To sum up, influence allows you to amplify every area of your life. You can make more money, have healthier and fulfilling relationships, get more freedom, and gain more control.

Whether you believe it or not, in the game of life, we are either influencing or being influenced by others.

If that's the case, doesn't it make sense to master influence? Yes, or no?

If your answer is yes, then this chapter will be of enormous value. It will unveil the secret that legends have mastered (consciously or unconsciously) and used as a weapon to influence others – be it one, or hundreds, or millions of people.

So, what's the secret to becoming a Master Influencer?

The secret to mastery of influence begins with understanding one fundamental principle, and that is:

You are NOT ONLY responsible for the words that come out of our mouth; you are also responsible for how the words land on the recipient. **And, here's the kicker: words do not land on the ears, but they tend to land on the heart of the listener/recipient.**

Have you ever said something to someone with their best interest in mind, but the other person got offended and did not take it in the right spirit/manner?

I certainly have.

The reason they got offended is that our words didn't land on their heart appropriately.

If you can successfully find your way to the heart and stir the emotions (positively) of your listeners, you can make an impact and influence them to take your recommended action. Whether you are influencing one or millions, that's the one fundamental secret that makes everyone tick.

If you can master this one single skill, you can master the art of impact and influence. Big News: Most humans are designed to take decisions based on their emotions and then justify them with logic.

Can we somehow master how to affect someone else's emotions positively? And what if your DNA isn't equipped with that talent?

The good news is, it's a skill, and it can definitely be learned.

But before we begin the process of learning, it is wise to understand and differentiate between the dark and bright side of influence.

THE DARK AND BRIGHT SIDE OF INFLUENCE

What does one do, when he wants someone to pay heed to his recommendation, but the recipient is resisting to do so?

In desperation, one may resort to coaxing, cajoling, bribery, blackmail, bullying and deception.

Is coaxing, cajoling, bribery, blackmail, bullying and deception also a part of influence?

Yes, it is.

Like every coin has two sides, influence also has two sides.

Let us dive deep and dissect to understand the different shades of influence.

There are 4 different ways in which people influence others to get the outcome they want. Let us take an example of a grid to explain the same.

INFLUENCE GRID

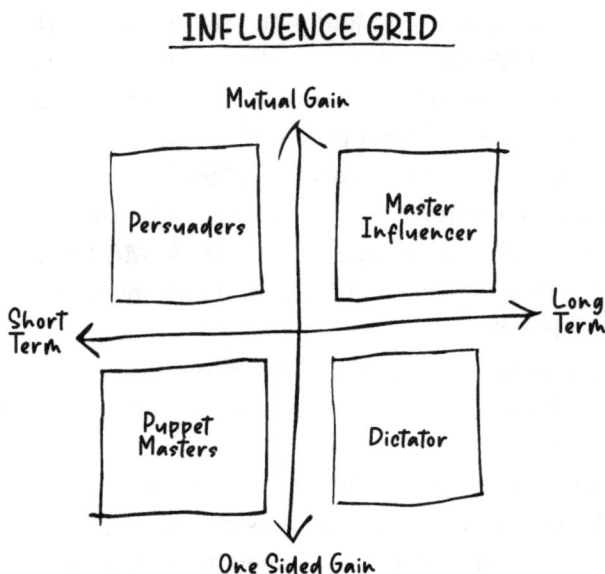

Mutual Gain

Persuaders

Master Influencer

Short Term

Long Term

Puppet Masters

Dictator

One Sided Gain

Dictator

A dictator is someone who uses his authority or position of power to get things done.

A dictator is not only limited to a ruler like Hitler who had total power over a country, but it can also come down to the level of your boss, your spouse or your parent(s). They use force or power to make you do things, whether you want to or not.

More often than not, a dictator can have control over you long-term unless you decide to blow the whistle and revolt out of frustration.

That's not what we are after because the audience will try to break free whenever they can.

Puppet-Master

A puppet-master is someone who manipulates others in a clever, unethical or unscrupulous way. They tend to apply pressure, power plays, and do anything required to get the outcome and satiate their needs.

All the puppet-master cares about is how to satiate his own needs. He wants to take advantage of people. The puppet master may resort to creating a false façade, where he exhibits that he is benefitting the other person, but in hindsight, it proves to be just the opposite.

A puppet master might succeed in the short term, but will rarely sustain his manipulations in the long run, as people understand when they are being taken for a ride.

We have all, at one point or the other, been victims of pushy and crafty salespeople, friends, colleagues or bosses. They used the dark side of influence to manipulate us to do something that we didn't want to, and we regret the action later.

What happens next?

They manipulated us and used us like a puppet once, but now we will be extra cautious around them as we do not want to be fooled again.

Maybe we did what puppet-masters wanted the first time, but we do not trust them anymore.

Persuaders

Persuaders get their outcome by compliance.

Compliance is when you get someone to act by altering their thought process, but you haven't changed their beliefs and values.

In other words, you got them to act in a way that they may not necessarily agree with and align to. The recipient may just comply because of external factors like social norms or short-term rewards.

So, what then is the difference between a persuader and a puppet master?

The answer comes down to one word – Intention.

The persuader uses influence techniques and strategies to get what he needs from his recipient by providing a certain value. Persuaders look for a win-win situation which benefits all parties involved.

Whereas the puppet master might use all the same strategies and techniques as the persuader, but he will do it with a one-sided view. A puppet master provides no value to the recipient at all.

Master Influencer

Master influencers, in contrast, are extremely powerful. They not only make you comply but also help to elevate you by altering your belief system and values.

A master influencer can impact someone's belief systems and stir the emotions of the recipient. They can successfully prime the recipient for a change that will undoubtedly last.

When one can indeed influence a person by converting his belief system, he can rest assured that the listener will fully buy into his message and follow them.

The listener will never doubt a master influencer because they look up to a master influencer as a role model or symbol for what they agree to and identify with.

In essence, one begins to share a common goal and identity with master influencers.

There's a big difference here and the other three sides!

That's what we are after - to become a master influencer – a force for good and a force for lasting change that sustains loyalty and raving fans over the long term.

We must consciously decide to master the ART and become a master influencer.

ART OR SCIENCE?

Now you may be wondering, why do I call influence a strategic art and not a science?

It is because not everyone has the same thought process, and not everyone behaves the same way. Hence, the same formula of influence doesn't apply to all.

So now the impending question is, "If everyone cannot be influenced in the same way, how does one learn and master the Art of Influence?"

Remarkably, though it's an art, it still has a strategy. And that's the reason I call it the strategic art of mastering influence.

> *Of course, you are interested in what you want. You are eternally interested in it.*
> *But no one else is. The rest of us are just like you: we are interested in what we want."*
>
> — *Dale Carnegie*

The fundamental strategy is to understand –

- **What motivates a person, and**
- **What specific needs does the person you want to comply have**

I know what you might be thinking: 'How would I know what motivates a person? I'm no psychic, therapist or psychologist!'

Let me explain. It's the understanding of a cardinal principle that drives all human thoughts, feelings, behaviour and actions, including yours.

So here it goes. Sigmund Freud, also known as the father of Psychoanalysis, suggests that all human beings are motivated by either of the two:

1. **The desire to avoid or decrease pain**
2. **The desire to create or gain pleasure.**

THE ULTIMATE MOTIVATOR

What Really Drives Human Behaviour

PAIN

PLEASURE

Move Away From
and Avoid Pain

Move Towards
and Gain Pleasure

It's simple but profound.

Let's reflect once: Isn't this the core basis of all the decisions we ever make?

Having said that, studies have demonstrated time and again that, when people have a choice, they will do much more to avoid pain than what they will ever do to gain pleasure.

This is what I call **P.O.P., i.e.; Pain Overpowers Pleasure**, which means that avoiding immediate pain overpowers gaining pleasure.

Picture this, when would you choose to run a red light – while you are running late to make it to a meeting on time on while you're running late to reach home for your favourite dinner?

More often than not, people will choose to run a red light to make it to a meeting on time to avoid the shame (pain) of being late.

The same feeling is echoed when people tend to avoid the immediate pain of going to the gym and following a healthy diet over choosing the pleasure of having a fit and healthy body for life.

Now that we understand the fundamental principle of what motivates or drives us, we must also be mindful of how our needs propel us.

R.A.I.N.B.O.W. – THE 7 HUMAN NEEDS

Anything that a human being does, he does it for a reason– whether it is getting married, building a business or getting a job, raising a family or travelling the world. He does it because it meets some of his needs. There is nothing a person does that is not an attempt to meet their needs.

My point is this: people don't go to work for the sake of the company. They go to fulfil their own needs. If the company can help employees meet their needs, the employees will, in turn, help the company get where it wants to be.

That's how an organisation grows.

If you observe how humans think, feel, behave and act, you would notice specific patterns. And all those patterns are trying to meet what I call the 7 fundamental and elementary needs of a human being.

Every person has these 7 needs in common. All behaviour and action – whether positive or negative – is purely an endeavour to meet those seven needs.

Needs powered by motivation are the driving forces that control why we do what we do. The urge to fulfil our 7 Human Needs is programmed in our nervous system. That's what our brain is doing and always going after.

Only after we're able to identify which human needs have been driving our listeners' decision-making, can we more accurately work to fulfil those needs. If we can meet their needs, we can get them to comply with our recommendations.

> 66 *There is a reason why the other man thinks and acts as he does.*
> *Ferret out that reason - and you have the key to his actions, perhaps to his personality."*
>
> **— Dale Carnegie**

We cannot win the game of influence unless we understand this.

I call these 7 fundamental human needs R.A.I.N.B.O.W.

Why rainbow?

Let me explain.

Have you ever seen a rainbow? Isn't it always an exciting and wonderful feeling to see a rainbow?

A rainbow is a rare occurrence in the sky when we can see a beautiful arc with 7 vibrant and distinct colours.

Because of its rarity, a rainbow has a lot of cultural and religious significance. It's a symbol of hope, inspiration, promise and good fortune. It is said that they break through dark places and lift us.

Human needs are quite similar to a Rainbow.

We too have 7 vibrant and distinct needs, and we get pulled towards them. Once our needs are met, they lift us and provide us with hope, inspiration, promise, and good fortune.

Let's discover what R.A.I.N.B.O.W. stands for:

R| Re-assurance

Envision an infant venturing away from his mother, but turning back frequently to make sure that she is still there. If the mother smiles back at the infant, the infant keeps going forward.

Why does the infant keep turning back to look at the mother?

It's because the infant is testing his current comfort zone. His mother's smile of re-assurance makes him believe everything is okay. The smile is a source of emotional strength that helps him to keep going forward.

The mother's smile of re-assurance makes him feel empowered to take a few steps further into the unknown, and to continue expanding his capacity. Without that re-assurance, he will come hurrying back to his mother.

We are not so different as adults, are we?

Certainly not. One needs re-assurance to feel safe and secure. Without a basic level of re-assurance, we feel threatened; and when we feel threatened, we tend to retreat.

Then again, if the need for re-assurance is fulfilled, we are more willing to extend ourselves like the child taking a few more steps when it could see the mother smile.

The need for re-assurance is the primary survival mechanism for us to function. It's our need to feel SAFE and to know what's coming next so we can feel secure. The need for re-assurance defines our level of risk tolerance; beyond which we will not venture.

Only when we feel secure at some level, we venture out to gain pleasure.

Simply stated, the need for Re-assurance is an inherent need for humans to avoid pain and stress, and also the need to gain pleasure.

Whenever you are trying to make an impact or influence someone, ask yourself, "What Re-assurance need does my listener have?".

A| Aspire to grow

> ❝ *The most pathetic person in the world is someone who has sight but has no vision.*"
>
> *— Helen Keller*

Every human aspires to grow in life by directing their hopes and ambitions towards achieving their vision of a better life.

It doesn't matter where one is in life right now; whether one is eighteen or eighty, whether one is flourishing and thriving at the highest level or struggling hard to make ends meet, this is a need that we all have in common.

We are born with a deep-rooted aspiration to grow and improve. If we are not growing and improving, we are not remaining stagnant. Instead, we are disintegrating and dying within.

Whenever you are trying to impact or influence someone, ask yourself, "What does my listener Aspire to be?".

l| Independence

> " A life without liberty is like a body without a spirit."
> **–Khalil Gibran**

The most fabulous gift our creator gave us is free will, i.e., the freedom to direct our own lives by making choices that are genuinely our own.

No wonder, we have an inherent and fundamental need to be free and independent. It enables us to express our identity in our relationships creatively, in the way we dress, and in our hobbies or line of work.

Independence gives a person the right to his fate and helps a person increase self-value and self-esteem. Being able to express ourselves freely is how we activate happiness.

On the contrary, if the need for Independence is suppressed and silenced by others, and one feels he can't speak up for what he wants, he starts to feel choked and suffocated.

Whenever you are trying to make an impact or influence someone, ask yourself, "Am I encroaching on his need for independence?".

N| Novelty

Visualise a situation where a child has two options in front of him, option 1 is to choose an old favourite toy, and option 2 is a shiny new toy.

Which one do you think the child will go for?

More often than not, the child will tend to gravitate towards the new toy.

Why?

The reason for this preference is simple – the need for seeking pleasure through Novelty!

Most humans will naturally gravitate towards Novelty, i.e. the state or quality of something new, exciting, unusual or unique with intense emotional sensations. They will go for it as long as it doesn't come with a perceived threat.

Brain research shows that a rush of dopamine, the reward chemical, is released when we experience something new. It is because we get bored by experiencing the same predictable things every single day.

Ask yourself, don't you feel the excitement when you experience something out of your routine? It may be meeting a new friend, learning a new skill, buying a new outfit/car/laptop/ phone or travelling to a new environment.

Life would be dull, and it would be impossible to thrive without Novelty. That's the reason we remember unusual days from our past (the day you got in trouble or broke up with someone or won the academic decathlon) better than the many other dull days that passed by without incident. The Novelty of those situations helped cement them in your brain.

Ultimately, people cannot maintain interest in any topic for long if Novelty is not present.

Novelty as a need for change and new stimuli is vital to our well-being that researchers have identified "neophilia" —

the desire to have novel experiences — as a predictor of longevity. People who actively seek out new experiences throughout life live healthier and happier.

Whenever you are trying to impact or influence someone, ask yourself, "What are his needs for experiencing novelty?".

B| Belonging and love

Belonging and love is the human emotional need to be an accepted member of a group. We need to belong to one another, our friends and families, our culture and country, and our world.

The need to belong and love is a strong and inevitable feeling that exists in human nature. It is primal and fundamental to our sense of happiness and well-being. It's a psychological lever that has broad consequences.

Being connected to other people and the need to belong may protect us from physical illness and emotional distress. Since we experience discomfort when this need is not being met, we seek belongingness throughout our lives.

The fact that belongingness is a need means that human beings must establish and maintain a minimum quantity of enduring relationships with someone or something.

Whenever you are trying to make an impact or influence someone, ask yourself, "What are his needs for belongingness and love?".

O| Obligated to care, share and give back

> 66 *I have found that among its other benefits,*
> *giving liberates the soul of the giver."*
> — *Maya Angelou*

Why do insurance companies play on this fear of 'what will happen to my family when I am not there', and build their sales pitch around the same to sell insurance cover?

The answer is straightforward.

Insurance companies try to encash on an implicit need of human beings. It's a need wherein we feel obligated to do more for others (whom we care about) than we will ever do for our own selves.

As humans we are hard-wired to do much more for others —for some people, it may be God, their kids, for some it's their friends, while for some it's their family, community or country.

Why else would a soldier give his life for his country, why else would Mother Teresa spend all her life serving others?

And you know what?

It is easy for people to settle once they attain a certain amount of wealth, achievement and respect. But it is the desire to serve and give to others, especially people they care about, that truly drives them to achieve more, no matter how great they are doing.

The desire to give our loved ones more compels us to keep moving forward and tap into our true potential. Let's admit this: only when you can provide an unconditional abundance to people you love or care about, that you experience true joy and fulfilment.

It all boils down to this: **Life is not about 'me', it's about 'we'!**

Ask yourself, what's the first thing you do when you get a piece of exciting news? I am sure you either call somebody you love and share it with them. Sharing enhances everything you experience.

Makes sense?

But hang on a minute. What about selfish people who only think about themselves? Do they not feel obligated to care, share and give back?

Of course they do. Even selfish people will go all out to do things for people they genuinely love and care about.

> " *The older we get, the more we realise that service to others is the only way to stay happy.*
>
> *If we do nothing to benefit others, we will do nothing to benefit ourselves.*"
>
> **— Carl Holmes**

Whenever you are trying to make an impact on or influence someone, ask yourself, "Who does he feel he is obligated to care, share and give back?".

W| Worthy of attention

> " *The deepest principle in human nature is the craving to be appreciated.*"
>
> **— William James**

Imagine that you are an excellent singer and you just performed your best piece in a packed restaurant. Sadly, after you have finished your performance, no one gives you a round of applause. How would you feel then?

Needless to say, you would feel bad. But why is it so?

You would end up feeling bad because the people at the restaurant did not pay any attention to your efforts in putting up a phenomenal performance.

As human beings, we have a need and desire to be worthy of attention. Everyone (from a child to a grown-up) needs attention like we need food. If there ever was any human who didn't need attention, they are now extinct.

We crave attention in forms of praise, respect, validation, acknowledgement, significance and/or feeling special, needed and important, or by being unique.

Seeking attention may seem like a disorder. To some, it may also seem controversial, but as corny as it sounds, it's a human need.

Think about it.

Why do people keep posting their beautifully edited pictures or their intellectual/humorous posts on social media? Why do they want people to like, comment and share their posts?

Why do people want to have fancy cars and latest and expensive gadgets? Why do people want to be billionaires and celebrities?

Why would people be collecting degrees that distinguish themselves as Masters or PhDs?

Why would someone put tattoos or piercings all over their body?

It is simply because of the inborn desire to be seen, heard, and noticed – in short, the need to be worthy of attention.

That being said, we all know or have heard of someone who says he doesn't like fancy cars or the latest phones. What about them?

Think for yourself, does that opinion get them some form of attention? I bet it does.

Fun trivia: The founder of Wal-Mart and the world's richest man from 1982 – 1986 drove around in a simple Ford Truck – F150. He could have chosen a Rolls Royce, a Ferrari or a Bentley or anything he wanted, but he chose a simple truck. Why? He felt driving a simple Ford Truck demonstrated he didn't need any of that luxury.

He quoted in his biography "I just don't believe a big showy lifestyle is appropriate". However, I sometimes wonder why he did have a private and personal fleet of fancy jets standing by!

If we could keep in mind that people need attention, it would change the way we see almost everything they do: from art to crime, from romance to terrorism.

Whenever you are trying to make an impact or influence someone, ask yourself, how can you make him/her worthy of attention?

WHY THEY DO WHAT THEY DO

Now, the question is, if we all have the same needs, then why do we differ in our behaviour and actions?

Here's the real deal.

First, everyone has all the 7 fundamental needs, but not everyone values all of the 7 needs equally.

Some may value significance and have it as their top need, whereas some may value belongingness or love as their top need. Whichever Need a person values as his number one priority will determine the path they choose to live their lives. And this path determines their ultimate destination in life.

Just imagine, would a person whose top need is 'significance' behave and decide the same way as another person whose top need is 're-assurance'?

Second, even if the same need drives two people, the means they choose to fulfil that need might be completely different.

Let's take the need to be 'worthy of attention' as an example. There can be two paths to gaining attention – productive and destructive means.

Gaining attention through productive means demands you to shine at your craft (whatever it is that you do)—for instance, being acknowledged at your workplace for achieving phenomenal results.

On the other hand, when some people get apprehensive and unsure of how to feel significant, they may resort to destructive ways to gain attention. Them may end up looking for sympathy (some may even go to the extent of deliberately hurting themselves to gain sympathy), or by creating significant problems that they know will get them attention.

Here's the thing, each of us has the same 7 needs, but each of us values and prioritise these needs in different ways.

Also, we can choose to meet any or all of these 7 Human Needs through different paths depending upon our values and beliefs. The hierarchy of needs and the direction we choose are why we differ in how we behave and act.

If it is so complicated, how do we know what's their most dominant need and influence them?

The answer is as simple as the question is complicated.

Simply ask them.

"What outcome do you want out of this?" or "What's most important for you to make this happen?"

But what if you are addressing a large audience and you cannot question them?

You must research and prepare to know your audience - who, why, when, where, and what they want. Know their desires and hopes, beliefs, values, wounds, and interests and then prepare a structure to win their hearts accordingly.

Structure to win hearts? Is there a structure that has been proven to work?

Gladly yes. And I call it the A.E.I.O.U.

A.E.I.O.U.

Does A.E.I.O.U ring a bell?

These are the 5 vowels of the English alphabet which represent the principal sounds of syllables.

Why are Vowels important?

You shall find a Vowel in every syllable of every word. They are the very life of words. They enable us to distinguish between words such as pant, pint, pent, punt or slip, slap, slop. If a child doesn't understand the vowels' sounds, they will struggle with reading and speaking.

What does A.E.I.O.U have to do with effective communication?

Just like A.E.I.O.U are the life of every word, the 5-step A.E.I.O.U framework is the life of effective communication. If we do not understand and implement this framework, we will struggle to impact and influence others. The 5 step framework is as below:

A | Awareness of wants and desires
E | Eliminate resistance and gain trust.
I | Initiate control.
O | Overcome Objection and Strategic Positioning
U | Urge immediate action

Follow this model for effective communication, and you'll be able to score a touchdown when making an ask. It doesn't matter whether it's pitching your business to an investor, getting a raise or even asking a friend/loved one for a favour.

Let's dive deeper to understand and implement the A.E.I.O.U framework to master the strategic art of impact and influence.

A| Awareness of wants and desires

Like almost everything else, influence too begins with awareness.

We must be consciously aware of the twin forces involved:

- What outcome do you want?
- What outcome does the other person want?

Your favourite dessert, maybe chocolate mousse. But, if you were to go fishing, would you bait your hook with chocolate mousse?

Possibly not.

The chocolate mousse cake is what you love, but the fish prefers worms, leeches, minnows, salamanders, and insects.

To catch a fish, it would make sense to hook your bait with what the fish prefers, yes or no?

Of course, yes.

Lloyd George, Great Britain's Prime Minister during World War I, managed to remain in power for a long time. There were other wartime leaders too, but people had forgotten almost every other wartime leader.

Was there a strategy involved to remain in power?

When an interviewer asked Lloyd George how he could man-age to remain at the top, he responded, "If my staying on top might be attributed to any one thing, it would be having learned that it was necessary to bait the hook to suit the fish."

What does it mean?

It simply means: **give people what they want, not what you want.**

This principle of awareness is critical in influencing others.

The most effective and efficient way to influence someone to do something that we want is to first frame it in terms of what will compel, drive and motivate them. To facilitate that, we must be able to see and understand things from *their* point of view.

We have to set aside our thoughts, opinions, and wants. We must also see things from the other person's perspective. Then and only then can we frame a win-win situation. That helps us convince the listener that it is in *their* best interest to do what-ever it is that we're suggesting.

WIN-WIN-SITUATION

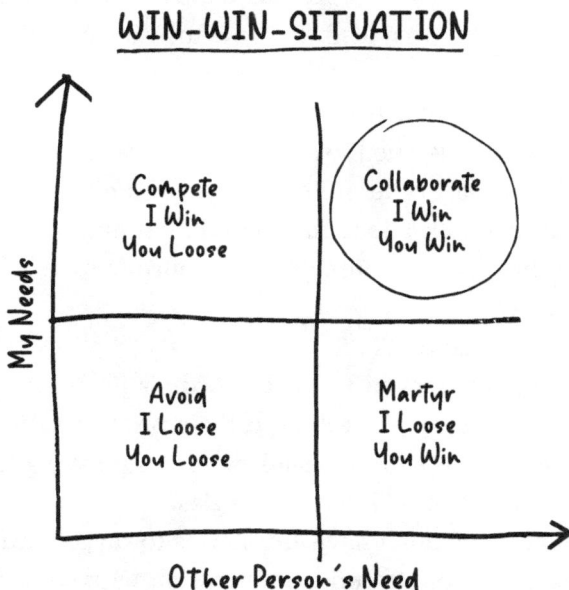

Compete
I Win
You Loose

Collaborate
I Win
You Win

Avoid
I Loose
You Loose

Martyr
I Loose
You Win

My Needs

Other Person's Need

The objective of awareness is to be mindful of a common goal with a win-win situation for all parties involved. We either ask them or plan about and research the same.

E| Eliminate resistance and gain trust

What do you do after the first step of being aware of what you want and what the other person wants and needs?

It would be wise to:

1. create a rock-solid foundation to eliminate any resistance from the listener and
2. get the listener to identify with you as a friend or an ally.

For you to influence the listener, you first have to gain his trust. It will help you convince him that you have his best interests in mind. It will then be easy for him to understand and associate with you.

The ultimate goal to gain trust is to make your listener relate to you. When your listener processes the message you're delivering, he should have a feeling of 'me too', instead of thinking 'so what?'.

But how do you illustrate that?

Have you ever listened to a speech by Barack Obama or Narendra Modi or any other influential politician?

They always talk about their childhood and the struggles they have had to overcome on their journey to reach where they are today.

Why do they do that?

Simply because when we listen to their problems, we feel they are just like us. We relate to their problems, and as we process the message in our head, we end up saying "Me too. Even I have had those kinds of struggles".

But what if you don't have any stories to say, or you are not on stage but in a one-to-one conversation with someone, can you not eliminate resistance and gain trust?

The good news is, yes, you still can.

You can eliminate resistance and gain trust by rapport!

Rapport is the ultimate power.

If you can master the art of developing rapport, you have the power to make other people responsive towards you. It can help you accomplish, achieve, manifest, or develop anything– be it personal, social, emotional, spiritual, intellectual or financial – much more rapidly.

The foundation of rapport is based on the principle that when people are like each other, they tend to like each other.

That's the key. When we think we have things in common with someone, we are more comfortable with that person. The more comfortable we are, the more we end up trusting the other person.

Sometimes, you may develop a good rapport instantly, while at other times, it may take some time and effort.

There are two paths to building rapport: the conscious and the subconscious. They can both influence others to trust you and your way of thinking, but each approach uses a different vehicle to reach its destination.

> *The royal road to a person's heart is to talk about the things he or she treasures most."*
> — *Theodore Roosevelt*

The conscious path uses words. Words are the pillar of any small talk. It may include questions about discovering where people come from, what they do, and sharing commonalities like their beliefs, values, past wounds, desires, hopes and interests.

When using the conscious path of building rapport, you must choose your words carefully. It must give the listener a sense that you are eyeing and working towards a common/mutually benefitting goal.

A common goal transcends difference of colour, creed, sex, culture, religion, or any other difference people may perceive as themselves having with you. A vision of a common goal eliminates all divides that may be present.

Also, be mindful to remember that people guard their opinions and beliefs with their lives, even if they are irrational or not true. For this reason, please do not provide any opinion that differs from theirs at this stage. Avoid debatable topics such as sex, religion or rival sports teams.

> ### The Ultimate Advantage Pro-Tip:
>
> Do not try to be the smartest person in the room. Make the other person feel they are the smartest. It can help you develop instant rapport, and you can get anything done from them.

But in reality, words and language are the least effective ways of building rapport as everyone has a different idea of what words mean to them. The real secret to developing massive rapport lies in how you subconsciously communicate with other people.

What do you think could be the common denominator of the best influencers in the world?

It's their ability to develop a rapport with anyone, from any walk of life, in literally a matter of minutes. They did it in minutes because they didn't just use words; they used other aspects of communication.

Albert Mehrabian, Professor of Psychology, proved in his research that 93% of how people feel and respond is governed by how you use your body. The balance 7% is linked to your choice of words. (We don't know if it's true or not, but why take a chance).

Hence, how you use your body is critical to eliminating resistance and gaining trust.

Let's get back to the topic about how the great influencers used the subconscious to build rapport.

They did it by behaving exactly like the other person – this is what is now known as **matching and mirroring**. The great influencers become a mirror image of the people they were communicating with – how they used their voice and their body. They would go on to the extent of making similar facial expressions and having similar posture.

You would now wonder, 'if we copy them, wouldn't they think we are mimicking them?'

Research shows surprising insights that people do not notice that. Instead, the listeners end up feeling wonderful because they think they can trust the other person. After all, the other person is just like them!

If you behave like them, they have no other option but to like you, because their brain tells them that you are a friend who is just like them.

Now, what are the things that you can match and mirror?

If they pick their nose, do you pick your nose too? Of course not!

Check how they place their hands and legs.

If they talk with their hands, you try to talk with yours.

If they sit cross-legged, you cross yours.

Try to be a mirror image of their body and attempt to engage their visual, kinesthetic and auditory senses.

Simply put, you go in and become a part of their world by being what they are.

Once you develop a rapport with someone for some time, you can then pace and lead them, i.e., you can make a subtle change, and the person will follow your lead. For instance, you yawn, and you will notice that they start to yawn.

It's pure magic.

Leading and Pacing brings us to the 3rd step, which is to initiate control.

The Ultimate Advantage Pro-Tip:

It will give you an unfair advantage if you could somehow give something valuable or do a favour first. People feel indebted and more often than not will tend to return the favour. But do not do a favour with the intention of getting something back. People are smart to catch on and may refuse to accept. Follow the 100-0 principle. Give 100% and expect 0%. You would be surprised to see how people reciprocate.

I| Initiate control

With your listener on your side, it is now time to initiate control.

What do I mean?

Do I mean you cast a spell on them and start to manipulate their mind, emotions and actions? No.

What it means is that you will now use all the knowledge that you have gathered in the awareness phase. You will use it as a weapon to reach the outcome, which is a win-win situation for everyone involved.

This phase aims to get a person to comply with your idea and get a soft yes in their mind, i.e., to get people to agree (in principle at least) to your request, even if they haven't come through whole-heartedly.

At this stage, you may put forward the core message that you want to get across. As an effective communicator, you may first give them a little logic and reason for them to justify the action. Presenting facts and figures up-front not only expresses your message clearly, but it also establishes you as a credible authority to provide the solution they seek.

And as you have taken out the time to prepare yourself, you will have an unfair advantage over every other person you interact with. You can now make everybody feel certain that their needs are being met.

But remember, just provide enough logic to trigger and justify the emotional decision. As informed earlier, people tend to make decisions on emotional reasons. But to feel intelligent; they always need to be able to justify the same with logic. It helps them believe that they are the master controller of their emotions.

But make no mistake about this: Logic makes people think. Emotions make people act. Put another way; logic makes people say, "I need to think about it", emotion makes people say, "Let's get started". It's your job as a master influencer to take them over the bridge from logic to emotion.

Beware: Most people do not like to be bombarded with statistics, facts and figures. As such, do not go into too much detail in your attempt to provide logic and reason. Otherwise, you risk killing the rapport that has been sustained this far. If you can, use humour or storytelling to provide the logic and reason in an easy and engaging manner. Combining information and entertainment is the master key to unlocking the engagement of your audience.

O| Overcome Objections and Strategic Positioning

    Before anything else, getting ready is the secret to success."

                                    – Henry Ford

Have you ever been in a room where everybody agrees with you 100%?

Sounds too good to be true, isn't it?

Great influencers mind-read and anticipate possible objections and overcome them ahead of time, unlike novices who react to objections as and when they crop up. This ultimate advantage is what separates the winners from the people who are hoping to win.

By anticipating and speaking out the possible objections your listeners could have, you demonstrate intelligence and empathy. It's one of the proven techniques effective influencers use to win people over.

But there are so many people and so many views. How can one possibly anticipate all objections to the recommended action?

If you observe carefully, all objections boil down to this:

- Is it easy?
- Can they do it?
- Does it work, and will it work for them?

If you can prepare and answer these fundamental questions, you will be able to tackle most objections, eloquently and elegantly.

For instance, while giving a sales presentation to your customer, you could say "A lot of our satisfied customers initially had questions like why is the price so high? Thus, to make the discussion more meaningful and enriching let me answer the same to you."

Any smart salesperson with experience would know that their product or service has some demerits or common objections. Instead of avoiding it, he may himself pinpoint the demerits and portray it as an advantage. For instance, he could say "A lot of our satisfied customers initially had inhibitions about our product being too bulky (the demerit). But once they started using it, they felt it only adds to the product being sturdier in the long run (the benefit)."

It makes more sense to overcome any objection in the prospect's mind while you are presenting the pitch, instead of them resisting you at the end.

If you miss this step, you will not be able to effectively convert them from a soft yes to an emphatic one.

The next thing you want to do is position yourself or your idea as the most logical choice if not the only logical choice.

How do you do that?

Research proves that people allow themselves to be influenced by you for the following two reasons:

1. You are an authority with a proven solution to a problem that they are facing. (If you have social proof to go with it. It will sky-rocket your level of influence.)

2. You provide an advantage or a scarce/limited opportunity to them. And you make them believe, if they do not go for your solution (product, service or idea), they will miss out on something.

The best way to position yourself is to provide an anecdote on how your life transformed from hell to heaven after implementing your recommended solution. The benefit of providing an anecdote is that it removes the doubt in the audience's mind and makes you seem more relatable simultaneously.

You can elevate your influence to the next level by highlighting the negative consequences of not following through or taking your recommended solution. This makes them more compelled than anything else. Remember POP (pain overpowers pleasure)? People will do more to avoid pain than to gain pleasure.

To summarise,

- anticipate and answer all objections while you are still pitching
- show them a vision of everything that can go wrong if they do not follow your recommended path and
- last but the most important, position yourself as the ultimate solution provider by showing a vision of everything that can go right.

This will prime them and provide enough momentum for the next logical and final step.

U| Urge immediate action

All the hard work you put into the framework means nothing if you cannot get your listeners to take the action you recommend – buy your product, care about a cause or invest their time or money.

In this final step, you finally ask and say what you want. You also highlight once again as to why the outcome you wish to achieve is mutually benefiting everyone involved.

If you have followed the framework and were able to communicate it well, then by this point, your audience would be almost sold to take the recommended action. You've left no stone unturned. You have made yourself the only logical solution by emotionally connecting with them.

Then again, most people falter at this step. They do not state the obvious. They do not ask for their listener to take action. They tend to assume that the audience will follow through anyway. However, effective influencers do not leave anything to chance.

They always ask for an immediate commitment by creating a sense of scarcity.

It could be something as insignificant as a phone call or an email address. Or depending on the scale of investment, a commitment on their money and/or time.

In personal communication, your ask might involve your partner checking with you before making a significant decision or being more gentle with you when you're upset.

Now you might say, "Koonal, I understand the need to urge them for action, but why does it have to be immediate?".

Have you ever heard of the phrase, out of sight is out of mind? What does it mean?

It means that you soon forget people or things that are no longer visible or present.

An effective influencer acknowledges the importance of the same. For that reason alone, an effective influencer urges the listeners/audience to take immediate action.

You don't want all your effort to go down the drain and start all over again, do you?

If not, then compel them to act immediately.

Now stop right there. Does it mean that we will always get the outcome we desire if we follow the A.E.I.O.U. framework?

Absolutely not!

It is almost naive to think that we'll always get the outcome we desire by implementing these techniques. But most people's experience shows that we are more likely to change attitudes with these approaches than by NOT using these principles.

Even if we increase our success by a mere 10%, we have become 10% more effective as leaders than before.

And with practice, it will become even more natural for us to apply these powerful principles every day.

The one key takeaway from this chapter is that we have a higher probability of getting our needs fulfilled if we go out and help other people fulfil their needs.

Now that we have taken out time to understand how to impact and influence others, I urge you to take immediate action and read the next chapter without further ado. I urge you not to lose momentum.

With a proper understanding of the next chapter, you will empower yourself with the superpower that somehow makes it 'impossible to fail'! Let's acknowledge and appreciate...

EIGHT

PROOF OF CONCEPT
The Magic Of Momentum Powered By Intelligence

❝ If the plan doesn't work, change the plan but never the goal."

— Unknown

Do you think the food at KFC is 'finger-lickin' good'?

If you don't know about KFC, I must tell you KFC stands for Kentucky Fried Chicken. It's headquartered in Kentucky, U.S.A., and is one of the world's most popular fast-food chains. As on February 27, 2020, it has 22,600 outlets in 135 countries and has annual revenue grossing over a whopping 25 BILLION Dollars globally. It is one among the world's Top 100 most valuable brands as per Forbes.

If you've ever visited a KFC outlet or have ever seen its hoarding, you must have noticed its logo. It has the face of a seemingly old man with a distinguished goatee dressed in a crisp white suit accessorised with a western tie string.

Who is he?

He is Colonel Harland David Sanders (popularly known as Colonel Sanders), the founder of KFC.

How did Colonel Sanders create such a fantastic brand with astounding success?

Of course, he was a brilliant kid born into a wealthy family and had the best education that money could buy! He got a degree in business and marketing from Harvard University (same university as Mark Zuckerberg – founder of the billion-dollar company called Facebook).

As Colonel Sanders had an abundance of capital and all the necessary connections with the right people, he headed straight out of university to work on his dream of selling franchises of KFC. He was fortunate to have been successful from the get-go. By the age of 65, he had retired with a fortune that would be enjoyed for generations to come!

What an entrepreneurial success story! Right?

Absolutely not.

What if I told you that none of the facts mentioned above is correct!

You would be amazed to know that he didn't end his career at 65; instead, he started to lay KFC's foundations when he was 65.

Now you may be wondering what compelled Colonel to keep going and achieve his dreams?

Well, at the age of 65, Colonel Sanders was broke and received his first social security cheque, which was for USD 105. He knew he couldn't survive on a meagre USD 105 a month.

Now, at the age of 65, most people would have cursed their life and said to themselves, "I'm too old, and everything is over". There's no point in trying to do anything at all.

But, the Colonel was different. While looking at the social security check of USD 105, he thought to himself, "How can I sustain myself and make a living out of this? What resource or skill do I have that I can use to make my life better?".

As he began thinking, he stumbled across the idea of selling his chicken recipe.

You see, at one-time Colonel Sanders owned a restaurant where he served chicken. The chicken recipe was his prized possession - a secret blend that he had created with 11 different herbs and spices. Anyone and everyone who ever tried his fried chicken, couldn't stop raving about it.

The restaurant was doing very well, but when the USA started preparing for World War II, it led to fewer and fewer customers stepping out. Thus, Colonel Sanders had to close the restaurant.

So here he was, looking at the social security cheque and thinking he would make a living by selling his proven chicken recipe.

But then, he told himself, selling a recipe wouldn't make me a lot of money. If I sell my recipe, my secret is out. I wouldn't get any recurring income as no one would pay for the same recipe twice!

It was then that he had a breakthrough which later changed the eating habits of the entire world.

He decided that instead of selling, he would franchise his secret recipe to restaurants that sold chicken already.

Simply stated, the Colonel wouldn't charge the restaurant owners for his recipe. Instead, he would provide restaurants pre-mixed packages of his secret herbs and spices. In return, the restaurants would give him a commission or a percentage of their increased sales due to using his secret recipe.

At the cost of sounding repetitive, I still urge you to think about it.

Colonel Sanders was 65 and retired. At that age, when most people would have given up and opted for the sanctimony of retirement, he opted to hustle and sell the world his secret chicken recipe!

Now back to his story.

As he had limited means, Colonel Sanders travelled door to door. He went to restaurants all over his local area in an attempt to partner with someone who would use his secret recipe and remunerate him with commissions.

He met restaurant owners who sold chicken and told them about his phenomenal secret recipe and how they could make the best chicken ever.

The Colonel tried to convince restaurant owners that by using his Secret recipe, their restaurant would be able to increase its sales exponentially. He also assured them that they didn't have to pay him anything upfront. He would give them the herbs and spices pre-mixed at no cost at all.

All the restaurant owner had to do was pay the Colonel a percentage of money that they made, *on every piece of chicken they ever sell, for the rest of their lives!*

What response do you think he got?

As with most start-ups, he was met with little enthusiasm and a lot of rejections.

Restaurant owners made fun of him as they thought he was crazy. They saw no need for the Colonel's 'Secret Recipe' as they already had a recipe of their own and were doing pretty well!

Do you think Colonel Sanders gave up after initial rejection and mockery?

Obviously not, that's the reason you still see KFC outlets today.

But the question is, how long did he have to keep on trying before he succeeded?

Legend has it that Colonel Sanders heard 1009 "no"s before he heard his first "yes".

Ok, let me repeat that.

He was turned down one-thousand and nine times before somebody accepted his franchise idea!

For nearly two years, he knocked on doors all day, only to go off to sleep with being rejected and mocked by others. And he would still be getting up the next day, with total commitment and passion for sharing his idea with someone new.

At this juncture, let me ask you a question, would you have knocked on the next door after being rejected a thousand times? Would you still have followed through on your dreams after having no success whatsoever for over 700 days?

How many times do you think you would be willing to fail before giving up on your dream?

Most people would have given up after 50 'no's, or maybe a 100 'no's maximum! They would have convinced themselves that their idea just won't work.

I am confident that like most people if we repeatedly fail, we too would convince ourselves that our dreams are not meant to be and give up on our dreams.

On the other hand, what do you think Colonel Sanders would have done if he didn't get a yes even the 1009th time?

Seeing his perseverance, dedication, and ambition, we can safely assume that he would have kept going forward until he got a YES.

Let's admit it; sometimes, this is what it takes to succeed in life.

Now, is Colonel Sanders' success after rejection/failure, a one-off case?

Decide for yourself:

Shah Rukh Khan was rejected in his early days as he was considered thin, brown and ugly. Shah Rukh later went on to reign over Bollywood and is often nicknamed the King of Bollywood.

Mahendra Singh Dhoni was rejected several times and found it hard to make it onto the Indian cricket team because he had an unorthodox batting style. Later he went on to win the world cup for India.

J.K. Rowling, the Harry Potter series author, was rejected 12 times before she was published. Eventually, she went on to earn billions of dollars for herself and the publisher.

A newspaper agency fired Walt Disney for not being creative enough. Also, his Mickey Mouse cartoons were rejected because they were considered to be too scary for women.

If that wasn't enough, "The Three Little Pigs" was also turned down because it only had four characters. To top it all, he was rejected by 309 banks, before a bank agreed to grant him a loan to create 'The Happiest Place on Earth' – Disneyland.

Today, millions of people have shared in 'the joy of Disney', a world like no other, a world launched by the sheer determination of one man.

You may find a common thread if you look at any of the legends in history, people whom the world considers most successful today.

What's that common thread?

While to the world, it may seem that the common thread is luck, it is not so.

As seen above, the common thread is the strength of the person in his beliefs and decisions, to the extent that they were unshakable when it comes to their drive, dedication and passion. They would not accept a 'no'. They would not allow anything to stop them from making their vision a reality. They wore an armour that made it impossible to fail.

At this juncture, it would be wise to conclude that it's not always the most brilliant who succeeds; but it's often the one who is most relentless.

Hey, enough of philosophy!

Let's be honest for a moment.

Failure is disheartening. And repeated failures inspite of giving your heart, soul and sweat can be fatal for the self-image. Failure has the power to make you stop believing in your potential completely.

Aren't you curious now?

What could be the secret sauce that made these legends persevere even after failing so many times?

Were they born with nerves of steel that didn't let failure demotivate them?

Were they cut from a different cloth that stopped them from quitting inspite of failing?

Would you want to know what the secret was?

The answer is life-altering, but it is very simple! So simple that I'm almost embarrassed to share it with you.

The answer is **MIND-SET**.

If you study the backstory of any achiever, you would know how many times he had to fail.

At the risk of sounding repetitive, I shall repeat it; Success is seldom a straight line. It usually has a lot of bumps in the form of rejections, failures and objections.

But successful people never saw setbacks as failures. They saw them as an outcome. If the outcome was different from what they desired, they saw it as a learning opportunity. They learnt from it and moved forward.

Now, this may sound esoteric and theoretical with limited practical implications. I get it! But, this is how it is.

Nobody has the power to keep going towards their dream despite failing numerous times. Failure is a baggage with heavy weight. It will undoubtedly slow you down. If you want to keep moving forward with the same momentum you set out with, you have to shift your mind-set and redefine failure as just an outcome.

If every time you try but fail, ask yourself, "What can I learn from it?", every attempt becomes a learning opportunity.

Hence, as long as you are learning, you are growing towards success.

It is this mind-set alone which makes it impossible to fail.

Whenever you fail, remind yourself that every sportsperson who is considered a legend has missed more goals/ more baskets/ more balls than they have ever scored. Whether it is Tiger Woods, Christiano Ronaldo, Michael Jordan or Sachin Tendulkar – the matches they didn't perform always outnumber the ones where they did.

For instance, everyone remembers Master Blaster Sachin Tendulkar for his 100 Centuries, but they rarely mention how many times he got out for a low score!

This is how the world works. The world has a habit of forgetting failures in the light of success. Do not treat failure as a setback. Just treat it as an outcome from where you can learn, grow and move forward.

Remember, you just have to click once!

But, wait a minute. If it is so simple, then how come everybody can't taste success?

That brings us to the 7th P – the key ingredient to successfully living an extraordinary life of having it all. I call it 'Proof of concept'.

PROOF OF CONCEPT

Do you know someone who knew he wanted, made a strategy to achieve the same and worked relentlessly towards it?

He was disciplined, determined, dedicated and desperate to achieve his goal. He kept pushing forward because he was confident that it would work out.

However, it somehow didn't work out.

What do they do next, if they too, were unshakable like Colonel Sanders, when it came to their drive, dedication, and passion?

More often than not, they would gather all their courage and go all-in again, giving every ounce of sweat they have towards accomplishing their target.

Yet somehow, they are still not able to make it.

After repeated failures, they feel that they have tried everything, but nothing seems to work for them.

That's when they transition from what I call **'D4+ to D4-'** i.e., from being disciplined, determined, dedicated and desperate, they shift towards being discouraged, disheartened, dejected and depressed!

What could be the problem here?

Sometimes, people who are focused on what they want, and continue to take relentless action get caught up in a pattern.

A pattern where one becomes fixated on their targeted outcome and obsessed with the strategies towards achieving it. They keep going all out and hammering with all that they have, without ever evaluating whether what they are doing is working or not.

Inevitably, after numerous failed attempts, they end up giving up on their dreams.

So many people do this all the time, right?

Its because they feel they have tried everything. But in reality, they got obsessed with their strategies. They kept on doing the same thing over and over again, expecting a different result. That's how Einstein would define insanity.

> *The definition of insanity is doing the same thing over and over again, but expecting different results."*
> — ***Albert Einstein***

Simply put, one may be aware of what he is capable of (potential story). He may be aware of what he genuinely wants (purpose). He may have the right psychology and be super productive. He may have mastered all the strategies of being in

Power State and may also find ways to influence others effectively, but he will not reach the desired destination if he keeps speeding up and gaining momentum in the wrong direction.

What does that mean to us?

It means, instead of always moving forward, we must sometimes pause and/or take a step back to measure our progress. We must be inquisitive and take Proof of Concept, i.e., evaluate if what we are doing makes sense or not.

Do you think Colonel Sanders kept following the same strategy as the one he started with? Or would he have taken proof of concept, i.e., taken into account and reflected upon what's working and what's not? I believe he would have frequently reflected upon his failures and incorporated the learnings in his sales pitch to improve upon his offerings to get the first 'yes'.

Sometimes a look back is a great way to leap forward.

I am an advocate of relentless action and getting things done. But the importance of looking back, and having a proof of concept is as crucial as the action you take to advance towards your long-term goals.

At this point, you should realise, every action you take might not necessarily propel you to move forward. We must take proof of concept by reviewing our processes, systems, values, and steps.

Isn't that what real intelligence is? To be able to differentiate between what works and what doesn't?

All in all, proof of concept is nothing but a fancy word for strategic reflection, which provides us clarity and perspective to deconstruct what works and what doesn't. Then and only then can we consciously choose to do more of what works. Do more of what brings results. Do more of what delivers. Do more of what moves the needle and moves us closer to our target.

Sometimes, when the results are not as per plan, all it takes is a small shift in strategy to get the momentum and the results you are after.

The most successful people maintain a focus on the present and take proof of concept whilst keeping their eye on the future. Proof of Concept helps make sure that the actions they take today are helping them move forward in the direction of their destination.

Remarkably, Proof of Concept is a philosophy and not a rigid framework.

It is less about relentless action, and more about thoughtful adjustments by accepting failure and incorporating learnings to perform better. It's finding out the way forward by asking focused questions.

For instance, if results are not as per expectations, you may ask yourself:

- What worked in your favour?
- What didn't work in your favour?
- What did you learn?
- What can you improve upon the next time?

Proof of concept is the alternative to the feelings of defeat and failure we experience after setting overly ambitious resolutions or goals, only to abandon them a few weeks later. Now, while Proof of Concept won't change your life overnight, it can bring about significant momentum (bit by bit) powered by intelligence.

That leads us to the last phase of our book. The Ultimate Success Formula, which I call A.I.R.

THE ULTIMATE SUCCESS FORMULA – A.I.R

This is where everything comes into play.

We've covered a lot in this book, but if I had to give you one key take away that I would want you to retain, it would be this ONE principle.

If you observe people who succeed, they have a strategy for what they do to succeed.

This strategy is a core principle for success. It doesn't matter if that success is in health, wealth, relationships, career, your interior world or any other facet that's important for you.

So you might want to highlight this and pay all your attention to this core principle for success.

The principle is simple, and it's a loop I call: **A.I.R – The Ultimate Success Formula**.

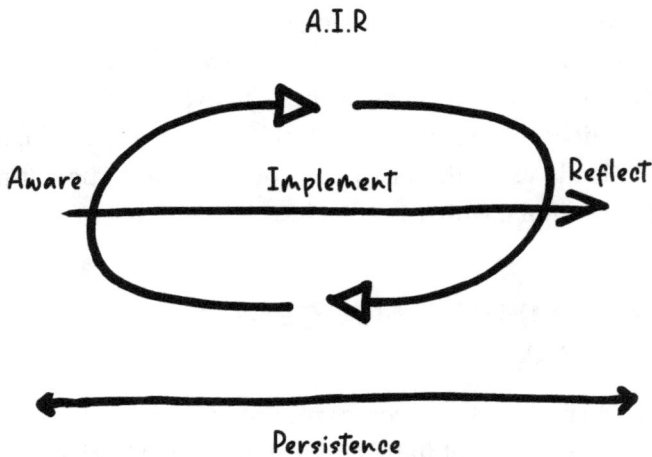

It can help you achieve your dream of living your Epic Life and live the extraordinary life.

So, what does A.I.R stand for?

A| Aware
I | Implement
R| Reflect

ULTIMATE SUCCESS FORMULA

A.I.R

Aware   Implement   Reflect

Persistence

Let's study them in detail.

A| Aware

The first step of the success formula is to be AWARE of what you ultimately want.

As discussed earlier, it makes sense to start with the end in mind. Not only that, you must know why you want it. The 'Why' is the drive that will compel you to keep going when things get difficult.

Isn't this what we extensively covered in the 5W framework of Productivity?

We know what we ultimately want out of life, why we want it, where we are in terms of getting it, what skills, knowledge, and habits we need to upgrade to, who can help us in our journey and last but not least, when are we going to achieve it!

Woohoo! We are now aware of our purpose and have provided meaning to our life. We are now mindful of the small goals/steps we need to take to reach the beautiful destination of our Epic Life.

But, does being aware mean anything at all?

Yes, and no.

Being aware is still 100 times better than living a meaningless Box-life, but it's still a hollow victory!

The key is to implement what we know.

That brings us to the second step of the formula, which is:

I| Implement

Inspiration without implementation is the biggest illusion.

Being Aware, i.e., knowing what you want and why you want it is an excellent start to pump you up, but it's not enough to help you realise your dreams.

You might get inspired by visualising what the future holds. But all your aspirations will remain aspirations, and all your visions will become hallucinations if you do not implement them.

Every single vision of your Epic Life, all the 'AHA!'-moments will produce positive change and bring about transformation only to the extent you implement. Your new life is governed by how you change your daily actions and integrating them into your lifestyle. That's what will produce results and help you live the extra-ordinary life you want to live.

All wise men in the past have agreed that nothing works unless we do the work.

What next?

It's the 3rd step of the formula, called...

R| Refect

We're well aware that success is seldom a linear and straight line. It will have a lot of bumps and curves which will halt your progress.

As such, it makes sense to take some time out to pause and reflect as you go along. Do not get caught up in the trap of implementing without measuring the effectiveness of your strategy.

The more you reflect, the more aware you know what works and what doesn't. It helps you let go of ways that don't work and implement more of what truly works.

It would be best to acknowledge that though the destination is fixed, the path is always flexible.

You keep getting aware, implement and reflect until you finally get what it is that you are after.

This infinite loop is the ultimate success formula, and anyone who succeeded in life applied this.

They may not call it A.I.R. – The Ultimate Success Formula, but they did apply it consciously or unconsciously.

Many instances exemplify the Ultimate Success Formula, but one that I would like to illustrate to drive my point home is of Thomas Alva Edison – one of the greatest and most prolific inventors the world has ever seen.

In his 84 years, Thomas Edison acquired a record number of 1093 patents. He was the driving force behind innovations such as the phonograph, motion picture cameras, microphones, the stock ticker, the stencil pen. And how can we forget his most iconic invention: the incandescent light bulb.

So how does A.I.R.: The Ultimate Success Formula relate to Thomas Edison's 1000s of inventions?

Let's inspect.

Was Edison Aware of what he ultimately wanted?

He was absolutely clear with his vision. Without being aware of what he wanted to invent, he wouldn't have invented such iconic products.

Did he implement it to make his vision a reality?

Oh, yes. Tens of thousands of experiments.

But, did he reflect on what was working and what wasn't and learn from it? Did he change his strategy to get the desired result?

You see, when people think of Edison, they tend to focus on Edison's numerous innovative ideas and creations which are no doubt legendary. But what many people miss out on is that, despite his outstanding success, he failed frequently.

Sometimes, it took thousands of attempts to perfect his experiments. One such experiment was when Edison was working to devise a new storage battery.

Edison had completed over 10,000 experiments with different chemicals and materials to develop his alkaline storage battery, and he still didn't have any breakthroughs. He never tried anywhere near that many materials in his invention of the light bulb.

In The authorised biography of Thomas Edison (by *Frank Dyer and T. C. Martin, Edison: His Life and Inventions*),

Edison's friend and close associate Walter S. Mallory narrates about the novel battery storage experiment.

Walter S. Mallory says:

> *"This [the research] had been going on more than five months, seven days a week, when I was called down to the laboratory to see him [Edison]. I found him at a bench about three feet wide and twelve feet long, on which there were hundreds of little test cells that had been made up by his corps of chemists and experimenters. I then learned that he had thus made over nine thousand experiments in trying to devise this new type of storage battery, but had not produced a single thing that promised to solve the question.*
>
> *In view of this immense amount of thought and labour, my sympathy got the better of my judgment, and I said: 'Isn't it a shame that with the tremendous amount of work you have done you haven't been able to get any results?'*
>
> *Edison turned on me like a flash, and with a smile replied:* **'Results! Why, man, I have gotten lots of results! I know several thousand things that won't work!'**

Hence, it is evident that Edison not only implemented what he knew, but he was also acutely sensitive and intelligent to reflect and differentiate between what works and what doesn't.

Not only that, it was the habit of reflection which led him to invent and patent over 1000 inventions!

How?

During one of Edison's early experiments, something went wrong. It led to an explosion that shook the workshop he was experimenting in. At the end of that, Edison gets up and starts reflecting and writing in his journal.

Later, when asked about failing and causing the explosion, he said, there was never any failure. Even when the experiment lead to an explosion, he discovered two things:

1. *A way that won't work*
2. *How to create a small explosion, which he may reflect upon later and might find useful when inventing something else in the future.*

Interesting, right?

I guess, he somehow knew the power of A.I.R – the Ultimate Success Formula.

What can we learn from Colonel Sanders, Edison, and numerous others who achieved success after many rejections and failures?

There is always a way if we are committed!

We just have to be aware of what we want and have a compelling reason to get it. We have to keep implementing what we know and reflect strategically to understand what works and what doesn't. And then keep changing the strategy until we can get what we desire.

The question is, are you committed to realising your Epic Life Vision?

If you are, then ask yourself, what level will you choose to play?

THE EXTRA-ORDINARY ANTHEM
[Adapted from Anthony Robbins]

> *I think it's possible for ordinary people to choose to be extra-ordinary."*
>
> —*Elon Musk*

Let's admit it; anyone who ever achieved anything phenomenal, never achieved it by playing at the level of 'Ordinary'.

Take a moment to ponder: What kind of results do you think people get when they play at the level of 'Ordinary'?

Ordinary, right?

Certainly not!

Most assume that people who play at the level of the 'Ordinary' can get ordinary results. That's certainly not true in the world we live today.

The world is too competitive. If one plays at the level of 'Ordinary', they are the first to get the pink slip and get fired or get eaten up by their competition. Remember: if you do an ordinary job, you either get poor or no results at all.

What's the next level people play at? It's called 'Good'.

So, what kind of results do people get when they play at the level of 'Good'?

Most people would say, playing at a level of 'Good' will definitely get you good results.

But, have you ever heard someone complain - I'm a good husband, or I'm a good wife; still, my spouse left me for someone else? Or I'm a good employee, why don't I get promotions at my job? Or someone says, I've always been a good parent, why don't my kids listen to me?

Most people are trying to play at the level of 'Good'; and, more often than not, people who play at the level of 'Good', end up getting ordinary results. It may seem unfair, but that's how life is wired. Good isn't good enough. Good is the new Ordinary.

If you are reading this book and have come this far, I am confident you won't be settling to play at the level of 'Good'. You are an achiever, and you want to make things happen, right? So you might want to play at the level most achievers play at!

Most achievers play at the next level, i.e., 'Great'.

So, what results do people who play at the level of 'Great' get?

Surprisingly, they tend to get good results!

What? Even when you play at the level of 'Great', all you get is good results?

See, when you are playing at the level of 'Great', you are one of the best. You get much better results emotionally, or financially in your career for being 'Great' than you would get at the level of good, but the icons and virtuosos play at another level altogether.

Playing at 'Great' gives you good rewards, and that's when most people become complacent and comfortable. We have all seen certain celebrities, athletes, business owners, etc. who reach a certain level and then stop.

Playing at the level of 'Great' brings comfort and seduces you to stay put. Comfort can be an emotion that can cause hindrance because when we get too comfortable, we stop growing, creating, sharing and adding value true to our potential.

The sad part is that they are so close to the level where all the phenomenal results are – the 'Extra-Ordinary."

Imagine yourself standing on the floor. The level of the floor is equivalent to playing at the level of the 'Ordinary'. The level of your waist is playing at the level of being 'Good'. The level of your eyebrows is the level at which the 'Great' play.

Quite a massive jump between those three, right?

Guess, where the level of Extraordinary is? The level at which people become icons, virtuosos and the heavyweight champion of their craft.

At the level of the forehead, that's just a quarter-inch above your eyebrows! It's that small a difference which enables you to stand out from the rest. You are only doing a little bit more than the people playing at the level of 'Great', but you get disproportionate and exponential rewards.

This might seem completely unfair, but this is how life is!

WHAT LEVEL WILL YOU PLAY AT?

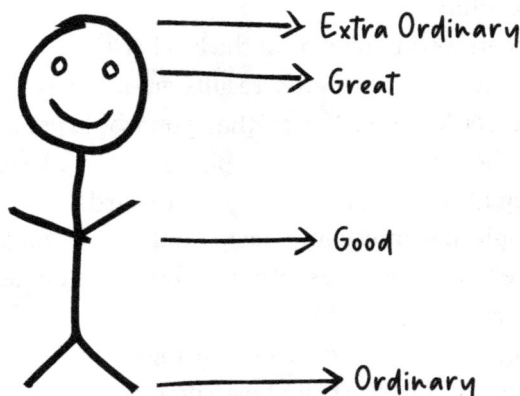

→ Extra Ordinary

→ Great

→ Good

→ Ordinary

This is the level we want to play at because when you are playing at this level, you reap extra-ordinary results.

Think about any sportsperson or business owner whom you admire for making it big.

Do you think they made it there by playing at the level of Good or playing at the level of Great?

There's no chance that you make it big and separate yourself from the rest by playing at that level.

They made it to where they are by demanding more from themselves and playing at the level of 'Extra-ordinary'. That's the reason they can reap extra-ordinary results, and that's the reason you admire and look up to them.

Extra-ordinary is the level where the Mother Teresas, the Mohammed Alis, the Nelson Mandelas of the world play at. They gain enormous respect and inspire us by simply exhibiting what a human being is capable of doing and achieving.

But what skill set do you need to learn to transcend from playing at the level of 'Great' to 'Extra-ordinary'?

The good news is, you don't need to learn any new skill set.

All you need is a small shift in your heart-set and mind-set.

Let me explain.

Do you know how one builds and develops drool-worthy biceps?

If you ask a gym trainer, he would maybe write on your exercise chart – Bicep Curls -10 repetitions × 3 sets and loads of other exercises.

In essence, to build biceps, you have to go to the gym and lift weights that curl your biceps. Also, you don't only lift weights, but you lift weights that stretch your muscles.

Long story short, you don't get drool-worthy biceps by going to the gym and lifting something comfortable for you. You build them by lifting weights that are much harder and make you uncomfortable.

If you do it, even though it's uncomfortable, and you keep doing it again and again, you build muscles. It's because the more you stretch and the more you demand, the more the muscle builds and expands.

Also, as a trainer would recommend, you don't just lift them once, but you repeat the curl at least 10 times in a set.

By the way, when you are stretching yourself and lifting weights, which one of those 10 curls do you think you would want to do the least?

Of course, No. 10!

And which one will give you the maximum muscle growth?

Number 13!

And you know what, ordinary people do only 7. They do it as long as it's easy and convenient for them and let go of the very moment they start to feel uncomfortable.

Good people do 10 because that's what is asked of them by their trainer. But, the people who play at Great stretch and hit 13.

And believe it or not, the people who have extra-ordinary biceps stretch themselves and hit 15 curls. They too want to give up when they hit 13. But, they do it anyway. They do it even when they feel they have no ounce of energy left and have given their all.

But the critical question is, how are they able to do it?

They can do it NOT because their trainer or someone else asked them to do it; they can do it because they demand more from themselves and because they refuse to give up. They want to test their limits and see what they are capable of doing. It's only because they are focused on the vision of how they would look and feel once they reach their goal.

The last 2 curls that differentiate the people who play at 'Great' and 'Extra-ordinary' are not due to skill or talent; it's their heart and mind, which makes them do it. That's how you enter the league of Extra-ordinary.

Hey listen: to shift from great to extra-ordinary, all you need to do is push harder and demand more from yourself than ever before. Take that extra step when you feel you've given all that you have and there is no ounce of energy left in you. The more you demand, the more you will expand.

Now maybe for you, it's not about having drool-worthy biceps. Maybe it's about being an extra-ordinary friend or an extra-ordinary father/mother? Maybe it's about being extra-ordinary at what you do on a daily basis. I don't know what it is for you.

Whatever it is, know that you are in charge and you get to choose the level at which you play. Know that you are in charge and that you can choose to play at the level of extra-ordinary and settle for nothing less than what you deserve. If you decide to play at this level, your whole life will change.

Don't forget that you will have to go through a lot of failures and rejections on your journey to realise your Epic Life Vision; you will feel exhausted and frustrated, you will want to give up. But, if you've got enough heart, enough vision and enough reasons, there's nothing you dream about that you can't turn into reality.

Your creator isn't dumb enough to give you the vision and not the necessary potential to achieve it. But you must have the heart, and you've got to play in the league of the extra-ordinary. That's how your life changes. That's how you make it all work for yourself.

Please do not get me wrong; when I urge you to play at the level of extra-ordinary, it doesn't mean being perfect. None of the icons and legends were after perfection because perfection is unattainable. Like them, we are after progress and not perfection.

What I mean by playing at the level of Extra-ordinary is to hold yourself responsible by setting a higher personal standard for yourself than anyone else would expect.

Now, you may choose to play at the level you are already playing at. You may prefer to continue to live life comfortably by keeping this book on the shelf, feeling all good and pumped up.

You might think this book was a good read, but that wouldn't change your life. You wouldn't be able to make your dream a reality. That would mean we've wasted our precious time together.

Because if you do not consciously decide to play at the level of Extra-ordinary, you might easily slip into habits, rituals, behaviours and attitudes or a quality of life that might be far below than what you truly deserve.

By playing anywhere below Extra-ordinary, you're doing your loved ones, who count on you, a massive disservice.

You're doing your community a massive disservice.

But most importantly, you are doing yourself a massive disservice. You are betraying the deepest part of you – your soul.

The greatest gift you can give to yourself and your family is to unleash the best version of you.

I urge you to consciously decide to play at the level of nothing else but Extraordinary. Remember, it's not a skill; it's a shift in mind-set.

So, that's the ultimate message of the book. Be extra-ordinary. Stretch yourself. Demand more from yourself and take massive, relentless action powered with the intelligence of reflection. Don't just do it for yourself, but do it keeping your loved ones in mind! Isn't that what an Extraordinary Life is all about?

No doubt about it!

We finally unearth the 7P's to Unleash your Ultimate Advantage, but there's just 'One More thing'. Without reading it and giving it the importance it deserves, the book might just be a sheer waste of your time. I call it the...

NINE

THE MIRROR OF HORROR
Beware Of S.A.F.E

❝ In the end, all or nothing will matter."
−Jay Mark D.

I tried my best to deconstruct and give you the psychology, strategies, stories, tools, and methodology used by achievers. It has the power to not only help you design but also live an extraordinary life.

However, knowing things intellectually is one thing. Going out and doing it every day is a different ball game altogether.

The Epic Life Vision has a unique characteristic of being exciting and scary at the same time.

Let's face it, there are lots of people who have great ideas. They get inspired for a moment on Monday, and by the time it's Wednesday, they have already given up!

Why?

It's because when you see your epic life vision, you see a lacuna and a big disconnect between where you are and where you want to be.

There will be times when the Negative Chatter Box (NCB) in our brains will start to see the risks involved in pursuing your Vision. It will make you want to go back to the S.A.F.E. harbour.

At this stage, it's very, I repeat, very very easy to give up.

This is what I refer to as the "The Mirror of Horror". The Mirror of Horror is what stops most people from living their Epic Life.

Let us go deeper to understand the 'Mirror of Horror' and give it the importance it deserves.

If we are eyeing something as big and monumental as our Epic Life Vision, chances are, there is risk involved.

Almost everyone will get scared to take the risk and want to go back to the safe zone. People will get scared because of the fear of loss, fear of going through pain and rejection, and fear of a negative outcome.

The Negative Chatter Box will start saying:

- Who do you think you are?
- You will never be able to make it!
- What if you lose it all?
- What if you can't do it?
- What if despite suffering all the hardships, you still can't get the desired life?

Remember: The Mirror of Horror has a unique ability to magnify all our emotional insecurities. It can completely superimpose itself onto our rational thinking.

One may give up when confronting the Mirror of Horror. Or at best, they may try to pursue the Epic Life, but when confronted with initial failure, they may want to run back to the SAFE zone and continue living the Box life.

SAFE is nothing but what I call Staying Away From Extra-ordinary (S.A.F.E.)!
Let me say this straight. It's a lot easier to stay in the Safe harbour of the known and keep thinking, behaving, and doing

what you've always done than to have the bravery to go out into the blue ocean of possibilities. But, we have to disrupt our old ways of thinking and behaving. We have to keep moving forward towards our Epic Life.

It's human nature to be frightened, so please don't think that I have conquered fear if I am writing this book. I am no different than anyone. I am also scared all the time.

But, as the saying goes, the cave you fear to enter holds the treasure you seek.

> " Being brave doesn't mean you aren't scared. Being brave means, you are scared, Really scared, badly scared, and you do the right thing anyway."
>
> — *Neil Gaiman*

People who achieved astounding success were as terrified as everyone else. They just installed the beliefs, the rituals and the routines to stretch themselves and keep doing things that scared them.

If you can gather enough bravery to get past that fear, if you cling on to your Epic Life Vision, if you continue to work towards it with faith, you will finally shatter the Mirror of Horror.

You will then embrace true freedom.

Of course, you will fail more than you think.

All throughout, we have seen successful people and super achievers failing many times before they succeeded.

We need to permit ourselves to fail. Because when we give ourselves permission to fail, we permit ourselves to fly.

If you get so afraid of failing that you never take the leap, then you won't fail, but you also won't ever fly. The key is to fail forward, i.e., learn from your failures to move ahead in life.

Choose not to retreat when the image you see in the Mirror of Horror is scary.

Choose to be brave and embrace your Empowering Potential story.

Choose to make your life a masterpiece!

Choose to be a model of excellence and resilience so that at the end of your life, you can appreciate and marvel at the life you've consciously lived.

As I say, there's always a choice.

Choose wisely and Unleash Your Ultimate Advantage.

This brings us to the end of the book.

> " *Now, this is not the end. It is not even the beginning of the end. But it is, perhaps, only the end of the beginning."*
> — *Winston Churchill*

I hope this book would have helped you with the specific tools and strategies required to shift you to positive momentum. I also hope that you will use this book as the foundation for building your Epic Life and that you will go back through this book whenever you feel like giving up.

I know for a fact that you have it in you to do what it takes to be successful. Because unlike many others who may have started but never completed the book, you were committed. You took the effort to finish what you had begun.

I sincerely thank you and applaud you for your deep commitment to learning and growing. I am ever grateful to you for allowing me to share the principles that I've found to be of enormous value in my life.

May you continue to imagine and dream beyond what seems possible at the moment. May you continue to dedicate yourself to being extraordinary and achieve more than what you've ever dreamt about. May you continue to live with enthusiasm and choose moments that truly matter.

I leave you with a quote from Walt Disney :

"If you can dream it, you can do it."

See you soon.

God bless.

KEY TAKEAWAYS

KEY TAKEAWAYS

KEY TAKEAWAYS

ABOUT THE AUTHOR

Koonal Jain is a passionate story-teller, a researcher and an eager student of human behavior. He is driven by a burning desire to make a difference in the world by inspiring and transforming individuals to unlock their peak potential and live a life they desire and deserve.

He is an M.B.A (specialized in Marketing), a certified Neuro Linguistic Practitioner (accredited by the American Board of NLP) and a certified Trainer (by Dale Carnegie USA).

At the age of 26, Koonal left his promising job in one of the world's leading Fortune 500 companies to become an entrepreneur and design the life of his dreams. He resolved to break-free from the limiting mindset, behaviors and habits that keeps us from living the extraordinary life.

Inspite numerous initial failures and struggles, today he is blessed to have achieved many significant life goals. Today he lives a life of meaning and purpose where he spends each day doing things he absolutely loves.

He is now privileged to travel all around the world and has also ticked some serious items on his bucket list like a romantic private yacht sailing in Santorini, an enthralling ziplining and quad-biking race in Fiji. He is now in the best shape of his life and feels fantastic to have evolved from a fearful, self-conscious and introverted man to someone who is confident and speaks effortlessly on stage to inspire others. And above everything else, he's delighted to have found enough time to play with and coach his daughter, and be the father he always wanted to be!

Koonal attributes his growth largely to his commitment to personal development through learning and modelling from people who have achieved astounding success.

He firmly believes there is always a choice, choose wisely!

www.ingramcontent.com/pod-product-compliance
Lightning Source LLC
Chambersburg PA
CBHW031620040426
42452CB00007B/593

9 781735 214122